Minnesota Celebrates Matisse

THE MINNEAPOLIS INSTITUTE OF ARTS

"What I am after, above all, is expression," wrote Henri Matisse in 1908. For several years before and many years after he offered this deceptively simple-sounding explanation of his artistic quest, Matisse expressed his bold vision in myriad forms—paintings, sculptures, drawings, prints, book illustrations, and cutouts. His output was prodigious and his contributions to twentieth-century art inestimable.

Both public and private collectors in our state have long been attracted to the lure of Matisse. His range of experimentation is represented in the more than sixty objects they have acquired and that largely comprise the exhibition "Minnesota Celebrates Matisse." For the first time ever, The Minneapolis Institute of Arts has brought together, from around the state, superb examples of Matisse's work, from oils on canvas to bronzes to prints and drawings. Each one confirms the creative genius of an artist who defies easy categorization.

In 1925 the Institute acquired *Woman with Folded Hands* (Fig. 3), the first work by Matisse to enter a Minnesota public collection. During the Depression years, local collecting of Matisse ceased, except in 1935, when the University of Minnesota Art Museum purchased the suite of six soft-ground etchings illustrating James Joyce's *Ulysses*. No Minnesota collectors or public institutions acquired other works by Matisse until after World War II.

With the arrival of Richard Davis in Minneapolis, first as chief curator and subsequently as director of The Minneapolis Institute of Arts, the local climate for collecting modern art changed radically. Davis persuaded the Institute to purchase two notable Matisse paintings, *White Plumes* and *Boy with a Butterfly Net*. He also encouraged local collectors to acquire important works by European modernists; as a result, Putnam Dana McMillan purchased a painting and drawing by Matisse, both of which entered the Institute's collection in 1961 as part of his bequest.

During the later 1950s the Walker Art Center acquired three Matisse lithographs. These were recently supplemented by the gift of *Reclining Ballet Dancer* from Judy and Ken Dayton. This lithograph, the first artwork Judy Dayton purchased, represents the continuation of a long Dayton-family tradition of collecting Matisse. In about 1962, under the aegis of Bruce B. Dayton, a life trustee of the Institute, the Dayton Hudson Corporation acquired ten Matisse bronzes from Carl Fredrik Hellström, the Swedish consul general in the Twin Cities; in 1971 the corporation presented five of these bronzes to the Institute. This largesse made the Institute one of the most significant repositories of Matisse's sculptures in the world.

Bruce Dayton has assembled an extensive collection of Matisse's works, with a strong focus on the graphic arts. He owns a number of the artist's illustrated books, as well as several prints, drawings, and the notable painting *Still Life with "Pensées" by Pascal*, one of the most subtle still lifes from Matisse's early years in Nice.

Other Minnesota collectors have acquired individual prints and drawings that complement the material in public collections in the Twin Cities.

Matisse As a Painter

Henri Matisse (1869–1954) is one of the giants of twentieth-century art. Pablo Picasso and the German Max Beckmann also had a tremendous impact on European modernism, but of these three only Matisse used color with such transcendent force.

Matisse, an assiduous student of both historic and contemporary styles, was inspired by the Old Masters and by the Post-Impressionist Paul Cézanne. Early in his career, he copied Old Masters paintings in the Louvre and through this process recognized the importance of certain themes that, for him, embodied the essence of Western tradition. In particular, still lifes, interiors, the pastorale, and the recumbent female nude, so fundamental to the repertoires of Old Masters and nineteenth-century artists, became his own preferred subjects. He repeatedly returned to these themes, refining and transforming them by stressing the primacy of color, elegance of line, and assurance of design. In his search for modernism, he concentrated on the two-dimensional reality of painting.

In his early still lifes and interior views, Matisse was already exploring the potential of color, experimenting with its intensity and glowing resonance. His unconventional use of color in the paintings he exhibited in the 1905 Salon d'Automne prompted one indignant critic to label him and his cohorts *fauves*, or wild beasts. This and other virulent criticism catapulted Matisse into the forefront of the avant-garde. Matisse sought the very essence of painting in his Fauve works. He previously had been inspired by Paul Signac and pointillism, a system in which juxtaposed dots of pure color were supposed to mix optically in the viewer's eye. Matisse soon abandoned this formal style and instead asserted the expressive and pictorial appeal of color, making it more than a mere component of design.

During the following year, Matisse produced works in which the significance of color became progressively more apparent. These pictures are composed of bold disengaged brushstrokes and patches of intense juxtaposed color.

By 1907 this liberating process took a decidedly different turn, as Matisse reduced his choice of colors and minimized the design element of his compositions. He applied paint more thinly over broad areas but did not sacrifice its intensity. *Boy with a Butterfly Net* (Fig. 21), one of Matisse's masterpieces from this period, was inspired by the artist's summer trip to Florence, where he was the guest of his friends and patrons Leo and Gertrude Stein in Fiesole. While in Italy, Matisse was particularly captivated by the frescoes of Giotto; he especially admired the way this medieval artist infused narrative with a power and clarity that proclaimed the dawn of Renaissance painting. What Giotto accomplished for painting within the strictures of the universal church Matisse hoped to achieve for modern painting.

His immediate response was to paint large-scale figures before a radically simplified landscape consisting of broad, uniformly colored zones of land under a cobalt-blue sky. In *Boy with a Butterfly Net*, Matisse captures the heroic grandeur and monumentality of early Greek sculpture; the figure of the youth, modeled on Allan Stein, son of patrons Michael and Sarah Stein, stands before a vast, empty landscape like a clothed *kouros*, or statue. The primeval background recalls the spare world of Giotto's frescoes. By returning to the very roots of Western painting, Matisse began a lonely odyssey to redefine the nature and validity of modern pictorialism.

The second picture from 1907, *Three Bathers* (Fig. 5), was a precursor of Matisse's celebrated—and considerably larger—*Bathers with a Turtle* of 1908, which is now in the Saint Louis Art Museum. *Three Bathers*, painted in Matisse's reductive style, is noteworthy for the thick lines outlining the figures; while initially reading as black, they actually resonate with unexpected color. These color shifts indicate how Matisse struggled to reconcile surface design with modeling in his quest to supersede the pioneering late paintings of Cézanne. Whereas Cézanne attempted to integrate many brushstrokes of color to emphasize the picture surface, Matisse reconciled design and subject matter in broader, simpler terms. He employed thick, undulating contours to compress the figures set within the wide horizontal bands of color that represent land, water, and sky. The modest scale of *Three Bathers* belies its importance as an early essay on the reductive mode that distinguished many of Matisse's greatest paintings, including the two versions of *Dance*, which are now in the Museum of Modern Art in New York and in the Hermitage in St. Petersburg.

White Plumes (Fig. 17), from 1919, is one of Matisse's finest paintings from his early years in Nice. His favorite model of the time, Antoinette Arnoux, wears an ostentatious hat designed by the artist. In creating this painting and other closely related pictures, Matisse produced a large number of drawings of Antoinette and other models sporting various dresses and hats. Together, these studies prefigure Matisse's most celebrated Nice theme— the partially nude, seated or reclining odalisque, inspired by his Moroccan sojourns of 1912 and 1913. Although these odalisque subjects were Matisse's most famous Nice-period pictures, the artist was also exploring two other themes in depth—still lifes and the interiors of rooms, usually containing a single figure.

Pictures from Matisse's Nice period reveal a movement toward a more broken and complex definition of space and a shift toward greater decorative design in the form of ornamental motifs. Whereas the reductive spirit of his paintings created before 1914 is still evident in *White Plumes*, with its restricted palette and bold isolation of the figure before the shifting red color field, many of Matisse's paintings from the 1920s display an overall surface design.

Yet in the mid-1920s Matisse painted a series of unpretentious still lifes notable for their concise design and discreet but glowing colors. One of these is *Still Life with "Pensées" by Pascal* (Fig.11), with its bold violet-colored orthogonal window recess and its blue-and-white jar filled with anemones. While not rejecting the decorative and ornamental character found in many contemporaneous Nice-period paintings, Matisse displayed in *"Pensées" by Pascal* a tautness of design that recalls *White Plumes* and even his most spare pictures painted before World War I. Matisse continued to draw inspiration from his early works, most dramatically when, late in life, he returned to this reductive mode to create his unique cutouts.

Matisse As a Sculptor

I took up sculpture . . . for the purposes of organization, to put order into my feelings, and find a style to suit me. When I found it in sculpture, it helped me in my painting.

Henri Matisse

For Matisse, sculpture complemented his painting. He began sculptural experimentation at the beginning of his career and returned to the medium off and on until 1950, a date that coincided with his last attempts at painting. Matisse created some seventy works, most of them small, freestanding bronzes of the female nude, cast in editions of ten from terra-cotta models. He generally made his sculptures for private study but also recognized their distinctive artistic qualities and included them in exhibitions as early as 1904.

By modeling his sculpture in clay, Matisse was able to experience volume and mass directly. He preferred working on a small scale so he could spontaneously manipulate the clay with his hands and gain a more intimate knowledge of the subject. And he concentrated on the most elemental volumes, integrating small components into the larger whole without devoting attention to descriptive detail. Because Matisse's sculptures frequently evolved parallel to his paintings, many of the abstracted and distorted figures represented in his canvases have three-dimensional counterparts.

Most of the Institute's sculptures date from the two periods—1900–1913 and 1923–32—when Matisse was most active as a sculptor. *Madeleine I* (Fig. 10), datable to 1901, was the first important piece that he completed and had cast. Its serpentine body bulges at the pronounced curving of the hip, yet this distortion seems naturalistic, given the artistic license Matisse took with the twisting body. Matisse inaugurates in *Madeleine I* the formal sculptural arabesque, the twisting and intertwining of body and limbs in space. In modified form, this arabesque recurs in most of his subsequent sculpture and relates to compositional issues that preoccupied Matisse in many of his paintings.

Matisse frequently produced second and sometimes third versions of certain sculptures. He either reworked an existing plaster cast of the original or began afresh in clay. Two years after Matisse produced *Madeleine I*, he sculpted a variant of this work. This practice of "serializing" while pursuing particular motifs or ideas was always part of the artist's creative process.

Even though the female figure became the most important subject in his pictorial art, until about 1900 Matisse had completed only a few figure paintings. *Madeleine I* and his other sculpted figures gave him the confidence to include figures in his paintings. After introducing them into his still lifes, the artist was able to focus on the figure as a major pictorial subject in its own right. In fact, Matisse often included his own sculptures as significant motifs in his still lifes and interiors, where they frequently resemble real human beings.

Matisse produced well over half his sculptures before World War I. The most significant works he made toward the end of this period are closely related to such contemporaneous paintings as *Boy with a Butterfly Net* and *Three Bathers*, and they share certain common stylistic traits with them. For example, vigorous contours accentuate the broad surface modulation that defines and energizes these sculpted figures and their painted counterparts.

About a third of Matisse's sculptures are portrait heads or busts. *Head of Marguerite* (Fig. 16), which dates from 1915, has a unique expressionistic power achieved by the forceful modeling of the gaunt head, combined with its distortion and asymmetry, and by Matisse's fusion of bust and pedestal. *Marguerite* seems to be more than just a portrait bust; it suggests a complete and intelligible figure—an existential head sitting upon a scrawny, truncated body.

The remaining three sculptures date from Matisse's second significant period of sculptural activity, 1923 to 1932. *Large Seated Nude* (Fig. 22) is the first indication of Matisse's desire in the mid-twenties to redefine his painting style—by infusing a more evident structure and by treating the human figure more monumentally. *Venus in a Shell I* appears at the end of this transitional period, after Matisse's painting exhibited these changes, whereas *Reclining Nude II* dates from a few years earlier, when Matisse's painting style was still in flux.

Apart from their important relationship to Matisse's contemporaneous paintings, these three works also reflect characteristics of Matisse's considerably earlier sculptures, such as *Madeleine I*. For example, they employ the three-dimensional figural arabesque. Seen from different angles, the powerfully contoured figures form startling silhouettes that vigorously interact with the enveloping space. To underscore this effect, Matisse often distorts his sculpted figures to enhance their expressive appeal. Even though he based his sculptures on close observation, each finished piece diverges from its source to a marked degree and becomes an autonomous aesthetic form.

Large Seated Nude represents a subject Matisse treated in several paintings, drawings, and prints from the first half of the 1920s. In this bronze sculpture, Matisse reduces the armchair to a minimal support. He also lengthens the torso of the body and stresses its angle of inclination to achieve a spatial arabesque. The completed sculpture conforms to Matisse's frequent practice of producing variations on a given motif: certain photographs document the existence of at least two earlier, destroyed versions of this sculpture, the first cast in plaster and the second in the original clay.

The three later sculptures in the exhibition demonstrate Matisse's joy in manipulating clay, whether in creating and distorting the curving forms of the body or in planing, shearing, and modeling its surfaces. His sculptures of this period exhibit a constantly changing and illusory appearance. In *Reclining Nude II* (Fig. 15), for example, the smoother forms of the body predominate in the front, but Matisse arbitrarily cut the clay in the back with a knife. He also boldly shaved off the looping arm to increase its angular silhouette and made small yet distinct gougings into the lower back, below the left buttock, and on the left leg. Matisse's artistic daring enriches our response to these sculptures, and his radical manipulation of the solid, transmutable substance expresses his resolve to redefine his art in all its forms.

Matisse As a Draftsman

Drawing is of the Spirit and color of the Senses.

Henri Matisse

Although Matisse is considered the greatest colorist in modern painting, he also was a master draftsman in black and white. He drew prodigiously, creating thousands of works in a multitude of techniques and styles. Whereas Matisse pursued sculpture and printmaking only sporadically and abandoned painting in 1951, he drew throughout his career.

Matisse always stressed the primacy of drawing in a young painter's training. And he compared his own preparatory work in drawing to that done each morning by "a dancer or acrobat . . . with several hours of limbering-up exercises." He recognized that the activity itself was helpful in coordinating the artist's eye, mind, and hand.

Drawing enabled Matisse to discover the "essence" of a motif. He produced various studies of a subject, "not to use in a picture—but to nourish me—to strengthen my knowledge." By making successive renderings of a single object, Matisse assimilated the external world, until the object he drew seemed a part of him. Such a process ended when he was able to "find a drawing that empties me entirely of what I feel."

For Matisse, drawing was a direct translation of emotion. Line drawing was the most expressive drafting technique because it was the purest and most simple, but the artist also recognized the expressive potential of shading. With charcoal he could explore both the essence of the motif and the nature of the surrounding light and atmosphere. Matisse often began by exploring a motif in charcoal and then moved on to line drawings.

Even in his paintings, which are now known mainly for their startling use of color, Matisse stressed the critical role of drawing. His Fauve canvases of 1905, for example, shocked viewers and critics because of their "bestial" brilliant and saturated colors, but Matisse explicitly stated the equal importance of drawing to these pictures. In fact, he considered such work as drawing with paint. Late in his career, when color seemed to reign supreme in the abstracted cutouts, Matisse likewise described the process of making these pieces as drawing with scissors. The primacy of drawing in Matisse's art is demonstrated in both the Fauve paintings and the much later cutouts. In the paintings the spots, dashes, and lines of color provide pictorial structure, while in the cutouts the contour lines of the distinct colored shapes enhance the power of these shapes juxtaposed or set against a stark white ground.

The five drawings in this exhibition date from around 1919 to 1948 and represent two major techniques the artist used—pencil and pen and ink. Regrettably, we lack examples of his drawings made with charcoal and with brush and ink. Drawing was such an important part of Matisse's production between 1918 and 1924 and during the 1940s that he was inspired to publish two albums—*Cinquante Dessins*, or *Fifty Drawings* (1920), and *Dessins: Thèmes et variations*, or *Drawings: Themes and Variations* (1943)—reproducing his drawn works.

Although *Reclining Nude* (Fig. 2) did not appear in *Fifty Drawings*, it is quite similar to works that Matisse included in this publication. Most of these meticulously executed pencil drawings depict a clothed or nude female, presented bust-, half-, or full-length. Using refined contour lines, complemented by subtle interior modeling, Matisse represents the isolated seated or reclining figure against the white ground of the paper.

Woman with Folded Hands (Fig. 3), executed in pen and ink, is closely related to a few works in *Fifty Drawings* of a model wearing a flowered hat that complements the decorative design of her dress. The exhibited drawing is a variation on Matisse's painting *Woman in a Flowered Hat*, which is closely related to the Institute's contemporaneous *White Plumes*. By truncating the figure's head in *Woman with Folded Hands* above the eyes, Matisse eliminated the very flowered hat that appears in the associated drawings and painting. This bold compositional effect combines with the fluctuating thickness of the pen lines and the vivid pattern of the dress to create a dynamic interaction between surface, space, and decorative patterning.

The Music Lesson (Fig. 13) dates from the early 1920s, when Matisse shifted from pencil to charcoal and stump, a process that enabled him to create shading by smudging with a pointed roll of fabric or paper. Simultaneously, his choice of subjects and the way he represents them are also different. Drawings from this period frequently contain more than one figure, and Matisse often depicts the setting in great detail.

Matisse's use of lithographic crayon in *The Music Lesson* is unusual, but the subject is closely related to many of his contemporaneous charcoal-and-stump drawings. Such crayon creates similar depth and atmospheric effects, but it cannot be smudged with a stump the way charcoal can. *The Music Lesson* is distinguished by subtle modeling and a delicate atmosphere. The forms of the two figures harmoniously reinforce each other, and the distinctive shape of the vase on the table complements the women's shapes. Although the figures face each other, their full-skirted dresses merge to form a larger generalized shape. These combined design elements produce a shifting emphasis between the women as real figures in an actual space and as dominant decorative forms within the already patterned pictorial field.

In the remaining two drawings, both from the 1940s, Matisse employs pen and ink to create images defined by relatively uninterrupted contour lines. They are associated with the production of Matisse's second drawing album, *Drawings: Themes and Variations*, in which works from 1941–42 are divided into seventeen series; each series is devoted to a different motif and generally consists of a charcoal study of the subject followed by line variations in pen or pencil. Once again, the artist moves from one medium—in this case, charcoal—to another—pen or pencil—in his examination of the motif. Matisse explained that in *Themes and Variations* he created "a motion picture film of the feelings of an artist," for no one variation was the "final," or definitive, synthesis of a given motif.

Woman with Still Life (Fig. 24) is close in date to the drawings of Themes and Variations. It reveals Matisse's continued use of pen and ink, and by incorporating certain motifs drawn from the works in the portfolio, it relates closely to them.

Leaves (Fig. 28), which dates from 1948, is one of forty pen-and-ink variations on leaves that Matisse executed in his garden or that of the nearby Villa Natacha, which belonged to his publisher friend Tériade. Matisse evidently divided the forty drawings into groups of different leaf motifs, each possessing its own charcoal theme study and succession of pen-and-ink variants. The ethereal Leaves reflects the artist's conviction that his line drawings were "generators of light." It also illustrates the more personal sentiment that Matisse expressed to his friend André Rouveyre in 1942 that "the drawing of the empty space left around leaves counted as much as the drawing of the leaves themselves."

Matisse As a Printmaker

I began to use pure black as a color of light and not as a color of darkness.

Henri Matisse

Matisse produced more than eight hundred prints, not counting his book illustrations. The prints in the exhibition represent all the major techniques he used, except drypoint. His printed work indicates how he exploited the innate physical qualities of a chosen medium. In executing his prints, Matisse used techniques that amplified his practices as a draftsman, and like his drawings, virtually all his prints are monochrome.

To him lithography, his major print medium, was equivalent to drawing; he was especially partial to transfer lithography. To create a transfer lithograph, the artist first draws on a sheet of paper an image that is then transmitted onto a stone; the final printed picture does not reverse the original. The technical processes of printing did not really concern Matisse; often he left the inking of intaglio plates or the pulling of proofs to members of his family, especially his daughter, Marguerite.

Marguerite stated that Matisse frequently executed prints after long and difficult painting sessions in order to create variations on a theme that currently interested him. His sensitivity to the potential of each printmaking medium enabled Matisse to produce almost exclusively variations of specific motifs through one graphic technique to the virtual exclusion of others. Two instances are the World War I series of still-life monotypes and the 1929 series of etchings devoted to the female model with a bowl of goldfish. Within each series, "subsets," such as that of apples on a plate in the case of monotypes and of the model's head and shoulders in the case of etchings, figure prominently.

Our single monotype, Three Apples and a Plate (Fig. 8), dates from the mid-teens, the only time Matisse used this distinctive technique: he scraped ink from the wet plate's surface to create a temporary image that resulted in a solitary printing. Of all the monotypes similar in size and subject, Three Apples is most notable for its broadly scratched contour lines, which give the fruit density while evoking a sense of almost infinite space. This image graphically illustrates Matisse's advice to his students to "always search for the desire of the line, where it wishes to enter and where to die away."

Many of the exhibited prints are lithographs from the 1920s, the period when Matisse explored this medium to its fullest. His dominant theme at this time is the studio nude, or odalisque, which he presented in an interior profusely decorated with exotically patterned textiles. Matisse had earlier created lithographs made up of lines, but he introduced a range of shading in many of the works from this decade.

Standing Odalisque with a Plate of Fruit (Fig. 14) and *Seated Nude in a Tulle Shirt* (Fig. 7) are examples of the latter approach; *Woman with Trifoliate Cross* (Fig. 26) demonstrates Matisse's continuing commitment to linear lithographs. In *Standing Odalisque* the artist sensuously models the figure's torso while simultaneously merging her and the other objects with the profuse patterning around them. Her upper body echoes the arch motifs behind, the skirt's decoration reiterates the flowered borders of the wall, and even the slippers, vase of flowers, and platter of fruit on the upwardly tilted floor seem to merge into the rug's ornamentation. *Seated Nude* reflects an interest in the contrast between the curves of the figure and the verticals and horizontals of the wall and floor. In *Woman with Trifoliate Cross* the figure's costume is elaborately patterned; playful curves dominate the foreground and distinguish it from the summary diaper pattern of the background.

In 1929 Matisse began to favor etching over lithography and produced almost half of all his etchings in this year alone, including *Face of Young Woman and Bowl of Three Fish* (Fig. 18). In this work the artist creates subtle correspondences between the forms of the woman and fish, using spare etched lines to capture the intimacy of scale and theme. Wisps of the woman's eyes and lips float on her face like the fish in the bowl and suggest a correspondence between the shape of the bowl and her head. Matisse left an ink film on the plate; when printed on the silvery China paper, this created a self-contained aqueous world set apart from the heavier white support.

Late in his career Matisse began to use linoleum cut and aquatint. In his linoleum cuts, as in his earlier monotypes, Matisse's drawn or incised lines remove that which will not be printed from the plate. In this process the white lines are isolated against the surrounding black printed surfaces. This inverts the traditional intaglio and lithographic techniques, rather like printing in negative. In the 1938 *Bowl of Begonias I* (Fig. 9), made the year he first used linoleum cut, the wide lines comprising the grid project it forward emphatically. Matisse counterbalances this grid by filling most of the composition with the curves of the bowl and leaves.

Matisse first experimented with aquatint in the 1930s, usually creating white lines on a black field the way he did in his monotypes and linoleum cuts. When he later extended his use of this technique, it most often was to make simplified portrait masks delineated by broad strokes against white backgrounds. One of the latest works in the exhibition, *Marie-José in a Yellow Dress* (Fig. 6), is the only aquatint and one of very few prints in which Matisse used colors.

Matisse As a Book Illustrator

I do not distinguish between the construction of a book and that of a painting.

Henri Matisse

In 1930 when the young Swiss publisher Albert Skira asked Matisse to illustrate a collection of poems by the French Symbolist Stéphane Mallarmé, the artist was already past sixty. Book illustration, which began as a minor interest, became an important outlet for Matisse's creative energies. He subsequently devoted most of his printmaking to illustrating texts, including beautiful editions of works by celebrated French poets of the Renaissance and nineteenth century. He created the majority of his editions in the 1940s, although some were not published until the following decade or even posthumously.

Matisse frequently spent years on the development of a book. His work on different texts often overlapped to such a degree that the ultimate publication date does not always reflect when he executed his illustrations. He oversaw all aspects of layout and design, including choice of paper and typography, sequence of text and image, and creation and incorporation of design elements, such as initials and ornamental borders. On a broader level, Matisse's work as an illustrator extended to designing frontispieces, book covers, dust jackets, and title pages for numerous journals, albums, catalogs, and programs.

In those editions where his involvement was total, Matisse disparaged "imitative" or literal illustration and saw his role as someone who beautifies or enriches the text. Rather than make exact transcriptions of the subjects described, Matisse would first immerse himself in the author's writing and then would create images from his own imagination that were analogous in theme and sentiment to the prose or poetry. From several variants on a given subject, he ultimately would choose the image that most closely reflected his response to the text. The final printed edition, therefore, represented only a small portion of the total output of studies and variations that Matisse had generated for each project. Most of his books illustrate poetry by a single author. In order to establish his own overall conception of text and design, he selected the graphic medium he thought best suited the general nature of the text he was illustrating and arranged the sequence of poems with his accompanying images.

Matisse's choice of authors to illustrate, based in large part on the discerning suggestions by publishers, enabled the artist to select themes that were already central to his art. Most notable among these were the gazing female face, the female figure, and nature as a sylvan idyll. As an illustrator, Matisse frequently treated these themes in an original manner. For example, some of his most radically abbreviated representations of the figure occur on the illustrated page. The evocative imagery of the authors whose work he chose to illustrate inspired Matisse to interpret the theme of idyllic nature in the most direct manner possible. In his illustrations of animals and dancing nymphs and satyrs Matisse freely explores the pastoral world through his imagination, even though he re-creates this world within his studio. Conversely, in his contemporaneous paintings he depicts nature only through windows, set beyond the self-contained universe of his domestic interiors.

The Institute is fortunate to own examples of all the major illustrated books by Matisse, as well as a variety of lesser projects in which his participation was more limited. For his first two important commissions— *Pasiphaé, Chant de Minos*, a work in prose, and the collection of poems by Mallarmé— Matisse approached the general problem of layout in similar ways, though the results are quite different. For each project, he sought to harmonize the relatively light and corresponding dark pages that faced each other. For the Mallarmé edition, the light page contained a full-page image, whereas the dark page contained text. On the other hand, in *Pasiphaé* the artist used black linoleum-cut images defined by white lines contrasting with light text pages.

Although Matisse began producing lithographic illustrations of poems by the sixteenth-century French poet Pierre de Ronsard (Fig. 12) before he began work on *Pasiphaé*, his edition of Ronsard was published later. In designing the Ronsard work, he took unusual liberties that represented a significant development in transforming Matisse's concept of the illustrated book. Different-sized images sometimes float alone within the wide-open spaces of a page, whereas others fill the space between the printed text and the paper's edge. Matisse occasionally places images of unequal size on facing pages, thereby introducing an unexpected new element of design.

Jazz (Fig. 25 and cover), dated 1947, is unique among Matisse's book illustrations and is a fitting conclusion to this discussion of his development as a designer of illustrated books. In a strict sense, it is not really an illustrated book, since Matisse did not begin with a pre-existing text; only after rendering his boldly colored compositions did he decide to create a handwritten script as a visual foil. Craftsmen used stencils to reproduce Matisse's original gouache cutouts by hand, and the result was a landmark in color reproduction. Many of the plates of *Jazz* are based on themes from the circus or theater, but in others abstraction prevails. In this book Matisse began to develop a repertoire of colored signs that reappeared repeatedly in his gouache cutout compositions.

Jazz represented Matisse's first major use of the cutout medium. Only occasionally had he previously employed it—as a technical aid in positioning imagery in his paintings and for the design of compositions reproduced as covers for journals such as *Verve*. Following *Jazz,* the gouache cutout was Matisse's major pictorial medium during the last decade of his life. Perhaps his initial disappointment at the discrepancy between his original compositions and their reproduced counterparts prompted this new interest.

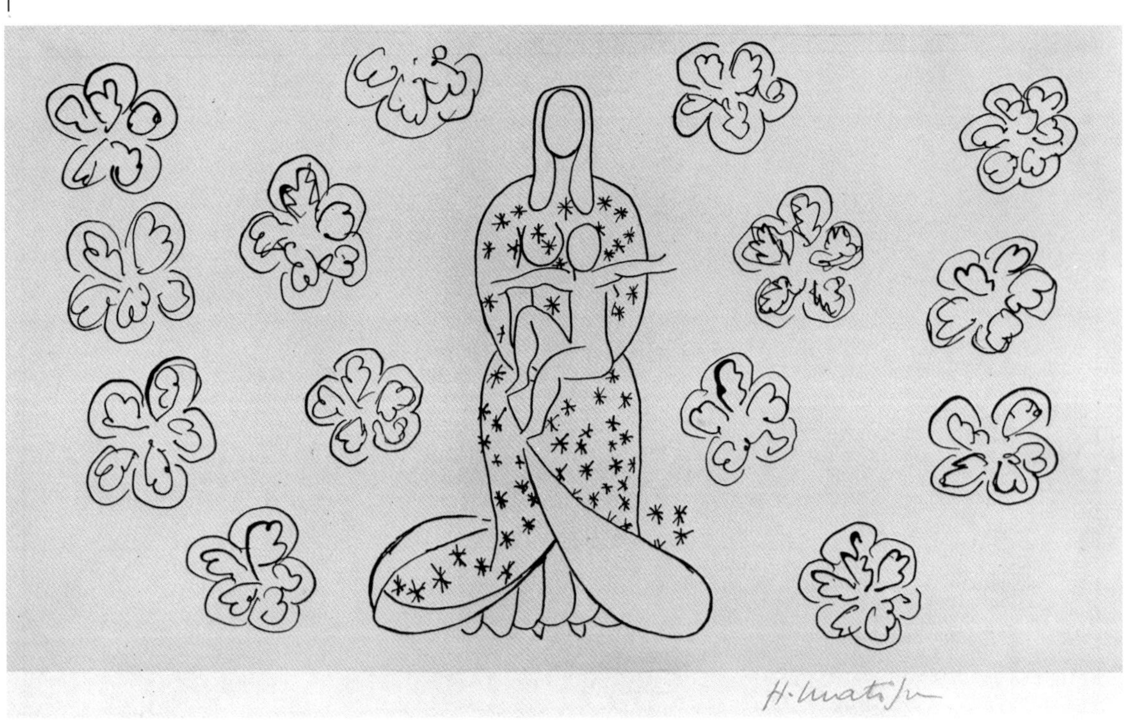

The objects in this exhibition range from the beginning of Matisse's personal quest for expression to the last years of his life. They demonstrate his undying commitment to discover and exploit the "purity of the means" in a wide range of different methods, as well as his inexhaustible energy and imagination.

Matisse stressed the underlying unity that distinguished his career when, late in life, he compared his cutouts to one of his finest early paintings: "As for *Le bonheur de vivre*—I was thirty-five at the time of this collage, and I am now eighty-two—I have stayed the same as when I created it. . . . all this time I have sought for the same ends, which perhaps I have achieved in different ways." At the same time, he revealed that his inspiration and sense of discovery were still as fresh as they were at the beginning: "You ask me whether my cutouts are an end of my studies? My searchings do not yet seem to me to have a limit."

Finally, Matisse's unquenchable zest and desire to explore, unceasingly, his favorite subjects are nicely summarized in this remark made in 1948 to his friend André Rouveyre: "I'm full of curiosity, as when one visits a new country. For I've never before advanced this far in the expression of colors. Up to now I've been tarrying at the temple gates."

George Keyes, Patrick and Aimee Butler
Curator of Paintings

Patrick Shaw Cable, N.E.A.-funded intern

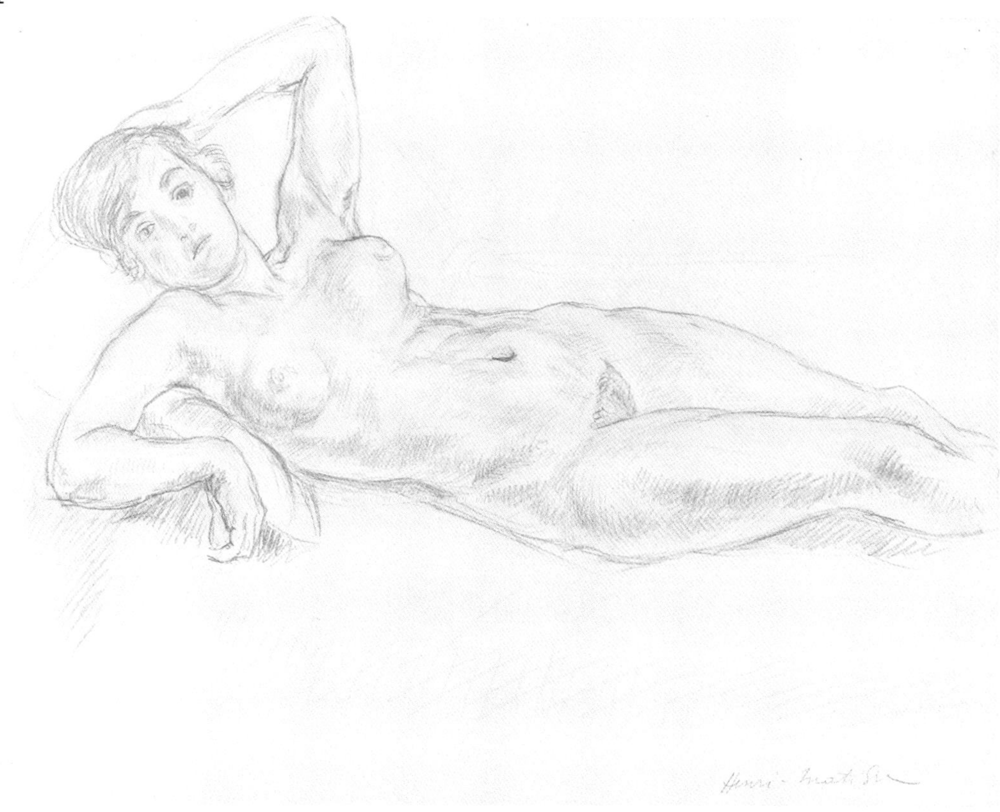

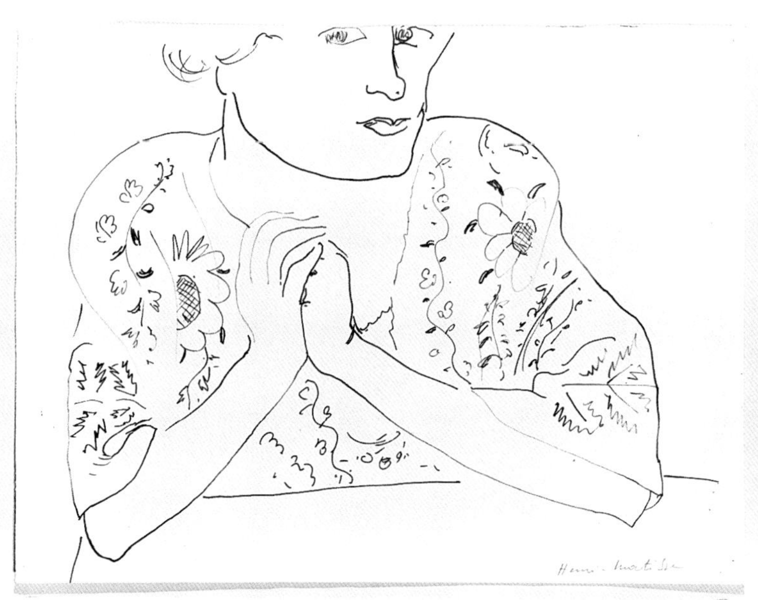

1 **Madonna and Child**, 1949
Lithographic reproduction of an
ink drawing
Collection of Ruth and Bruce
Dayton

2 **Reclining Nude**, about 1920
Pencil on paper
Private collection

3 **Woman with Folded Hands**,
about 1919
Pen and ink on paper

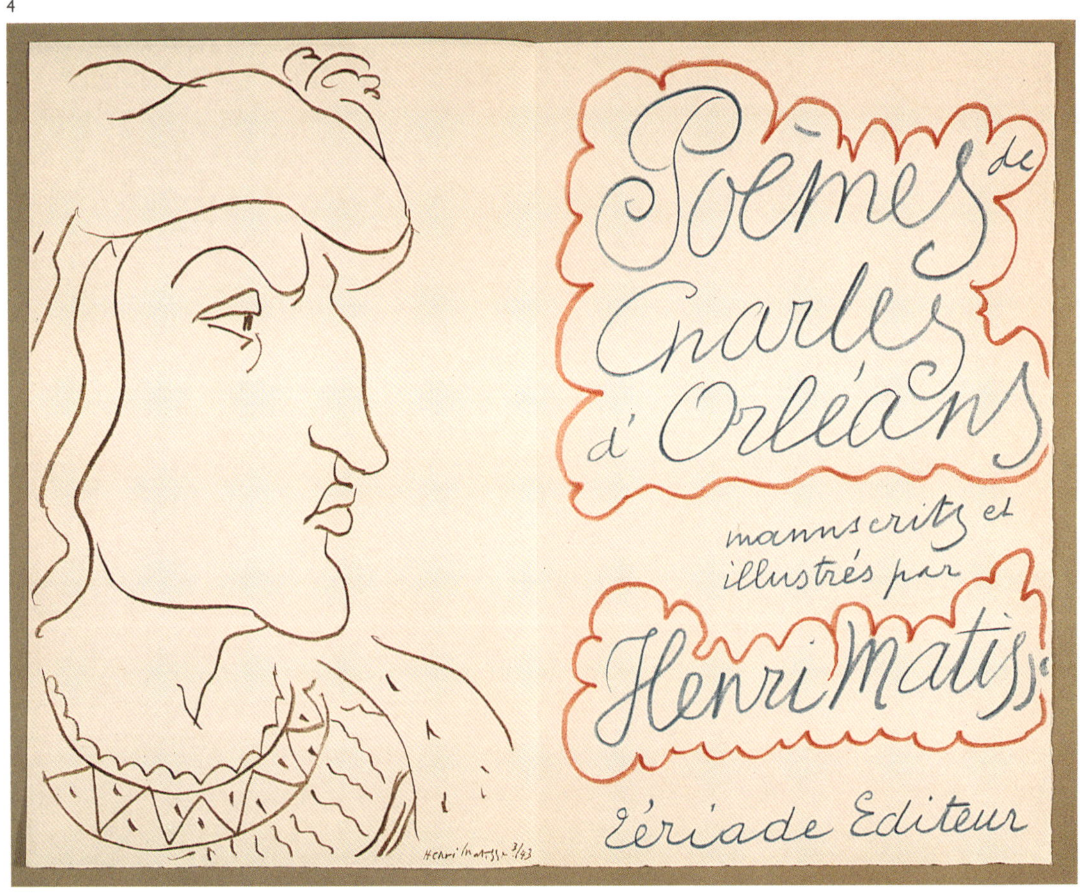

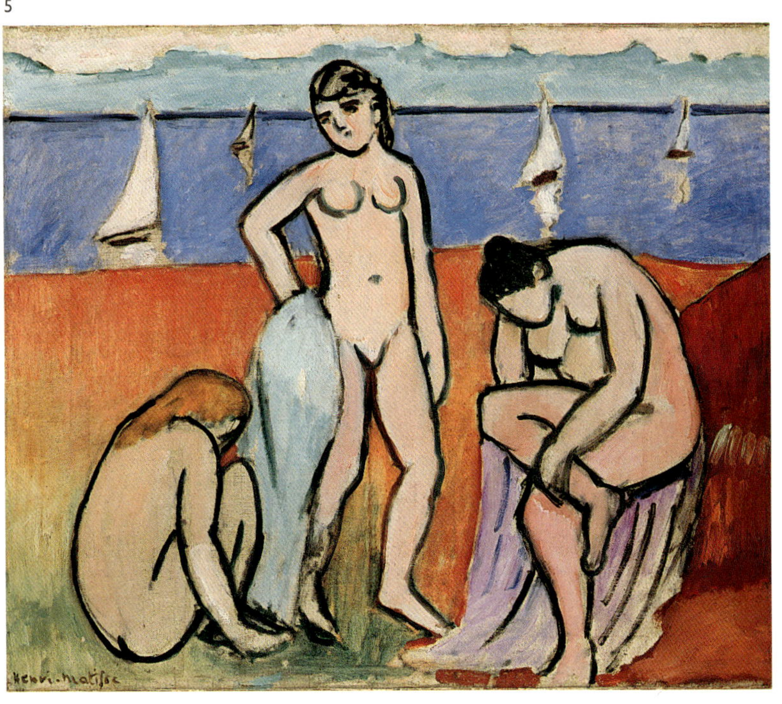

4 **Frontispiece with Author's Portrait** and **Title Page**, from Charles d'Orléans's *Poèmes*, 1950
Lithographic reproductions of colored-crayon drawings

5 **Three Bathers**, 1907
Oil on canvas

6 **Marie-José in a Yellow Dress**, 1950
Colored aquatint
Private collection (formerly collection of Donald Winston)

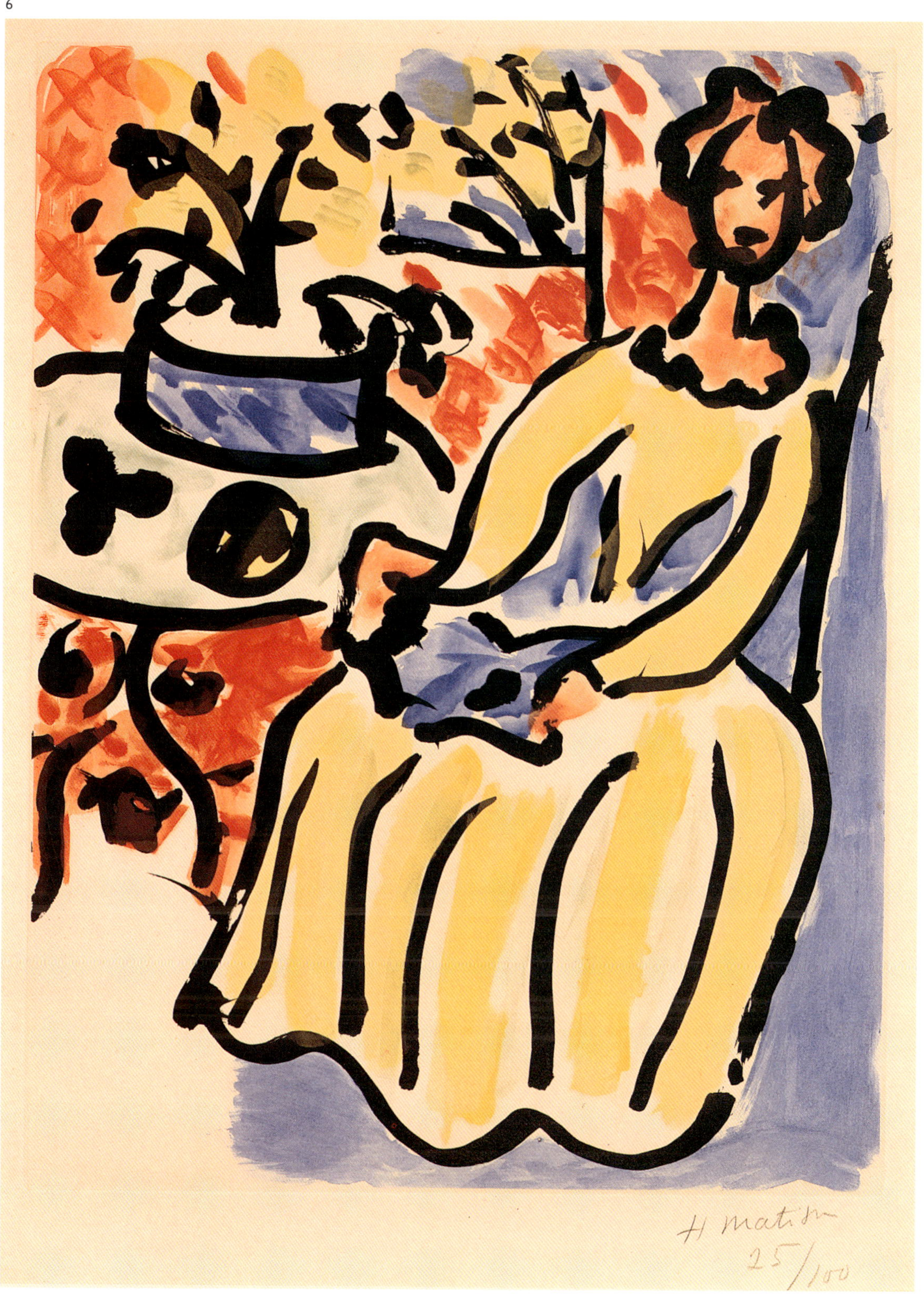
H. Matisse
25/100

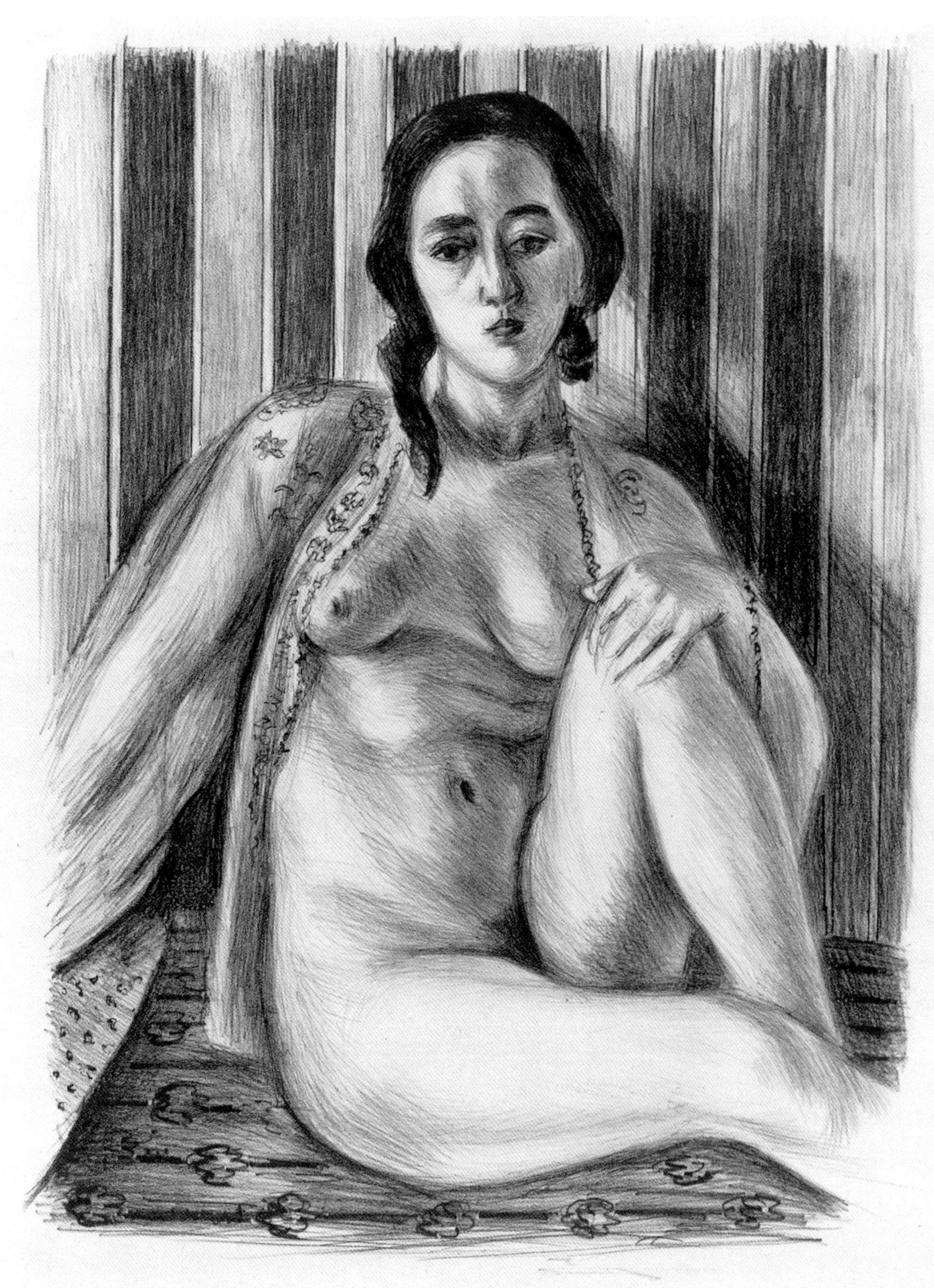
Henri-Matisse 6/50

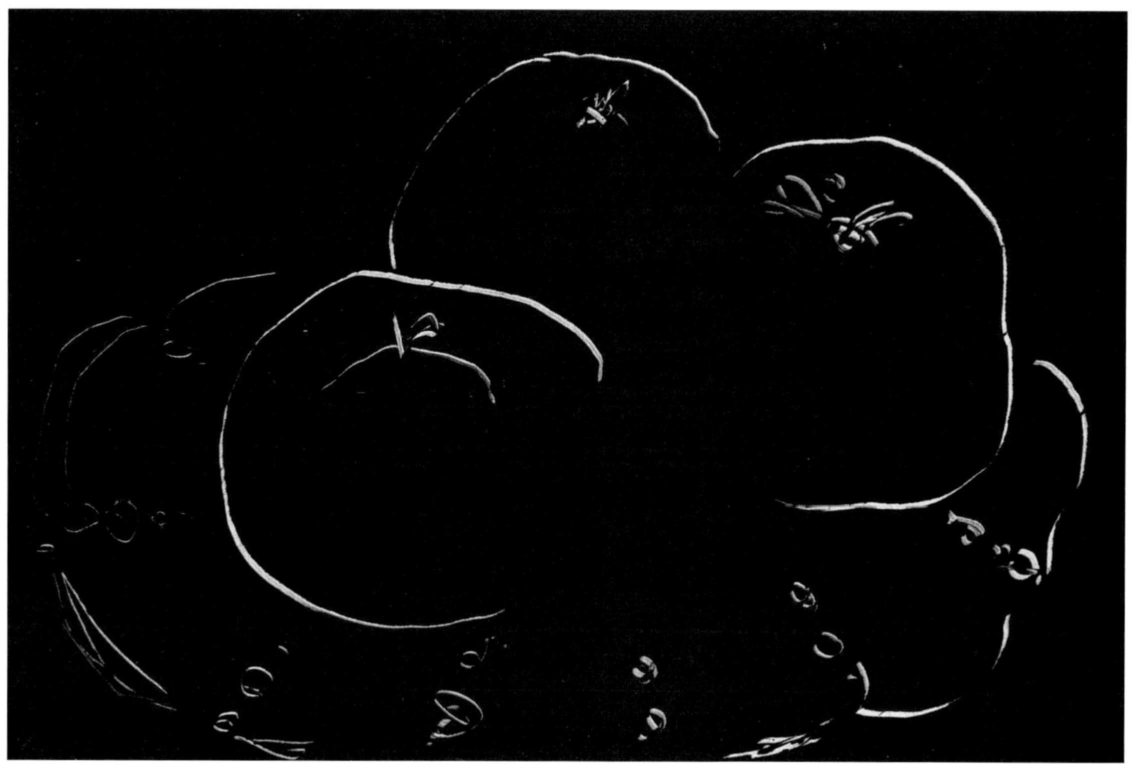

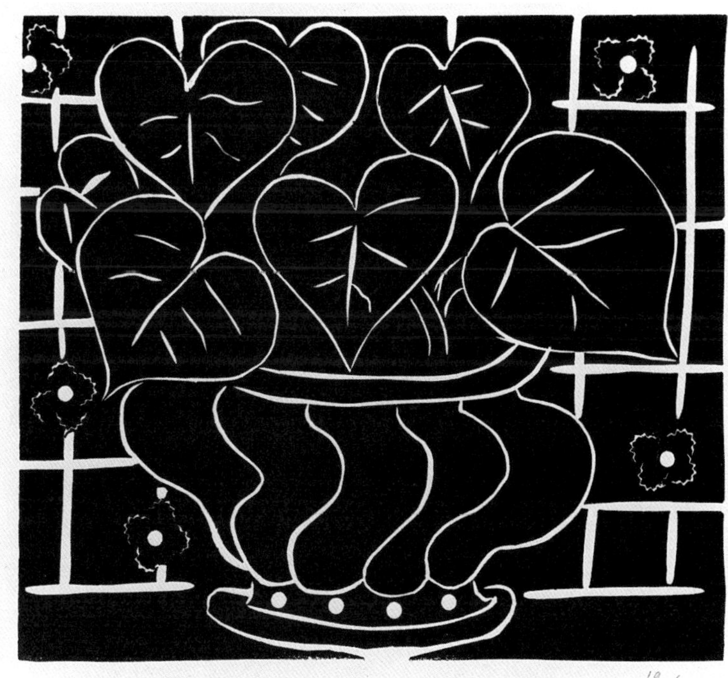

7 **Seated Nude in a Tulle Shirt**,
1925
Lithograph

8 **Three Apples and a Plate**,
1914/15
Monotype

9 **Bowl of Begonias I**, 1938
Linoleum cut

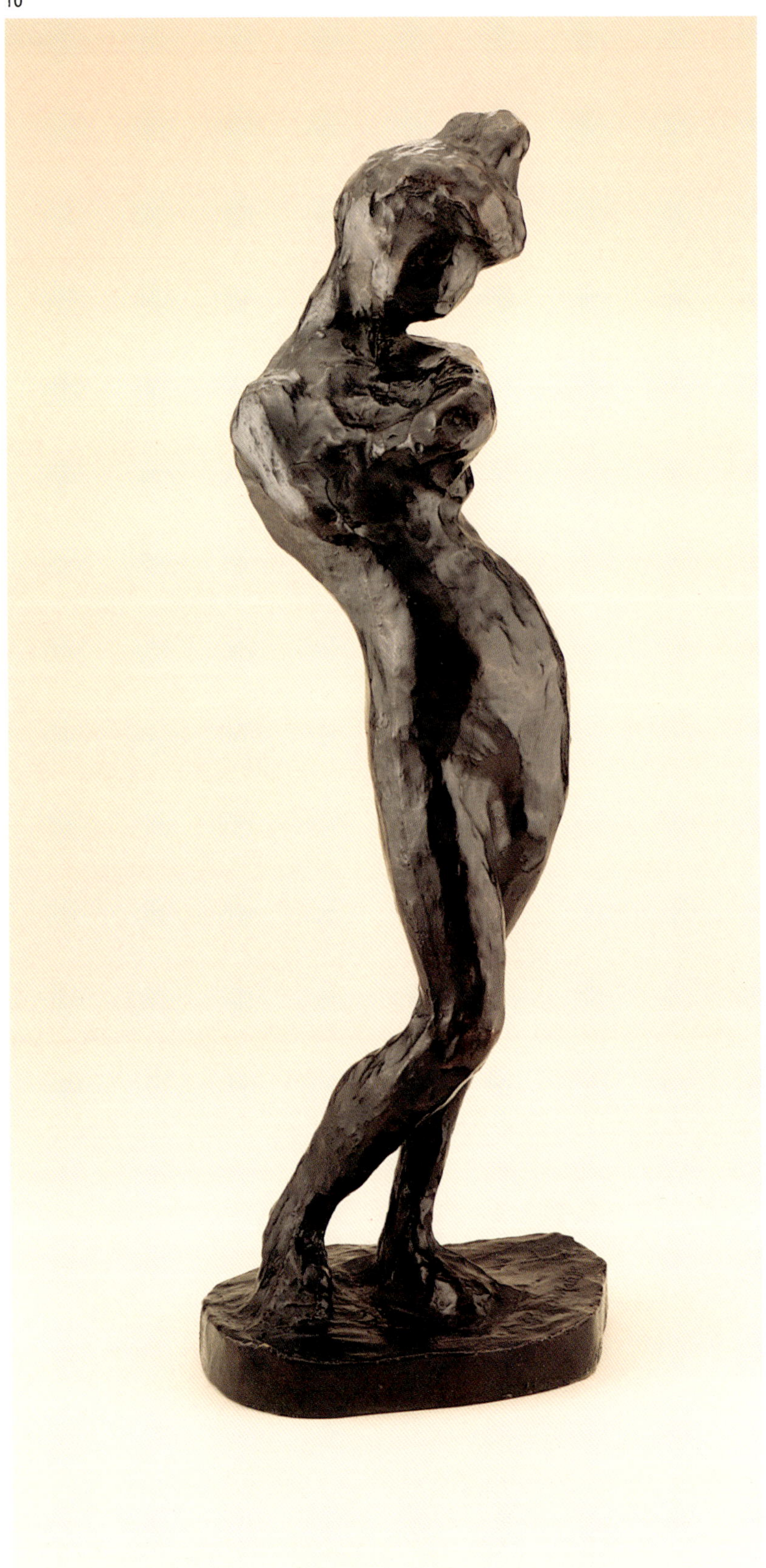

10 **Madeleine I**, 1901
Bronze

11 **Still Life with "Pensées" by Pascal**, 1924
Oil on canvas
Collection of Ruth and Bruce
Dayton

12 **Bird** and **Vase of Lilies**, from
Pierre de Ronsard's *Florilège
des Amours*, 1948
Lithographs

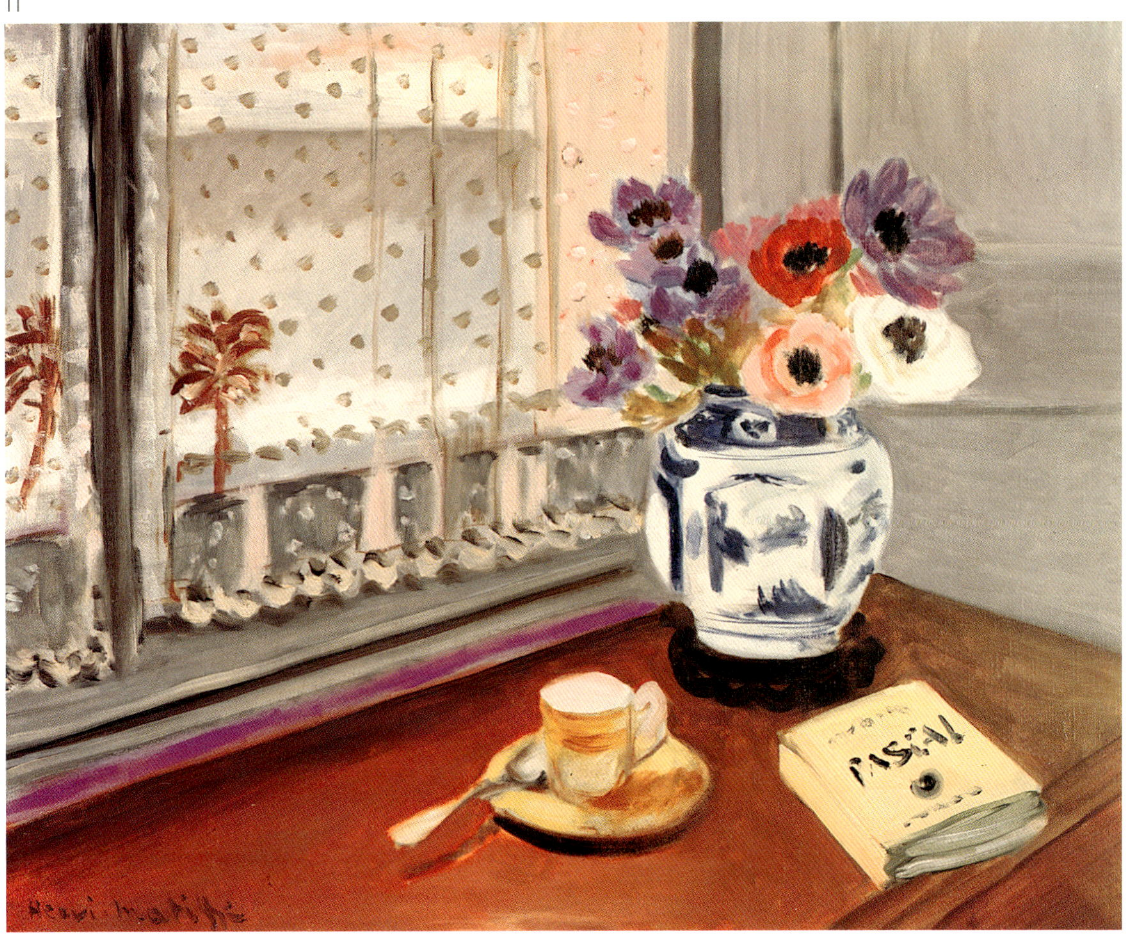

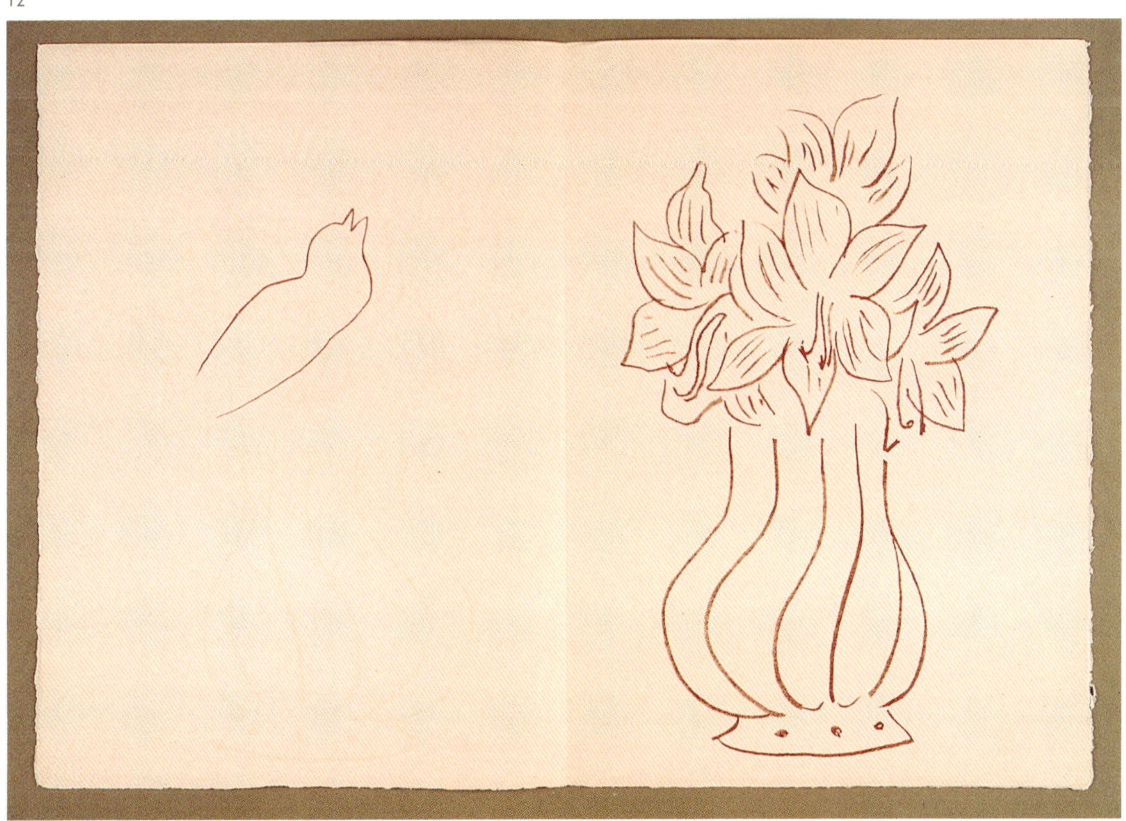

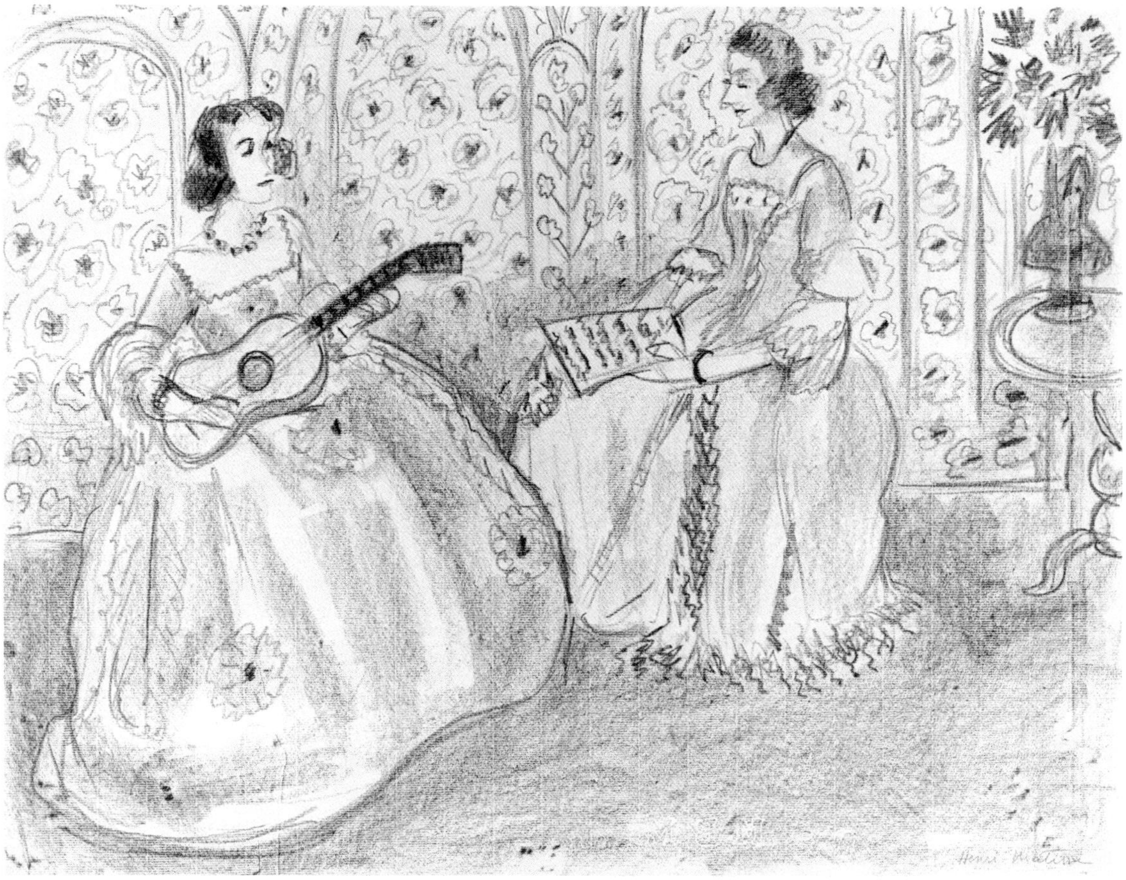

13 **The Music Lesson**, about 1922
Lithographic crayon on paper

14 **Standing Odalisque with a
Plate of Fruit**, 1924
Lithograph

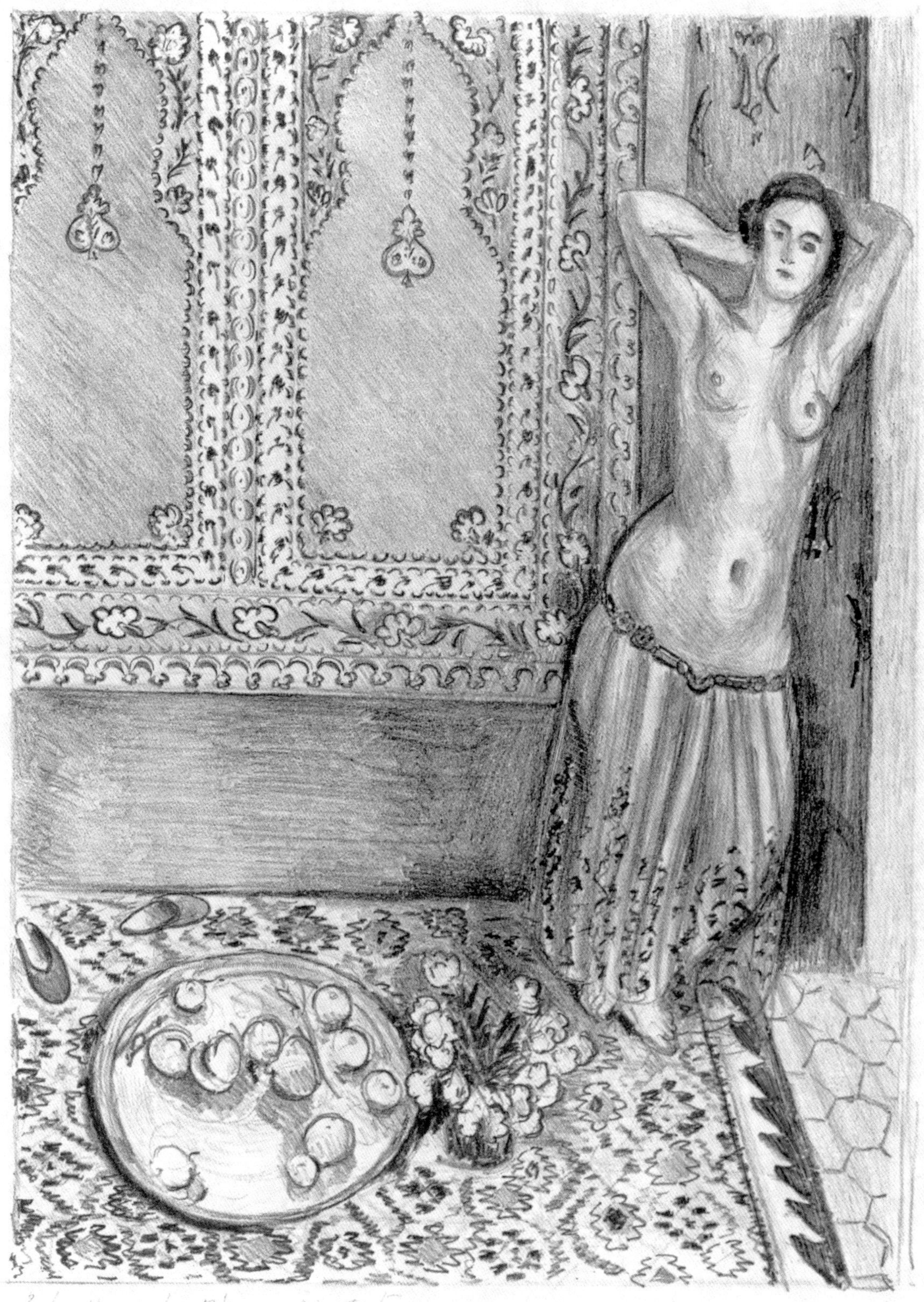

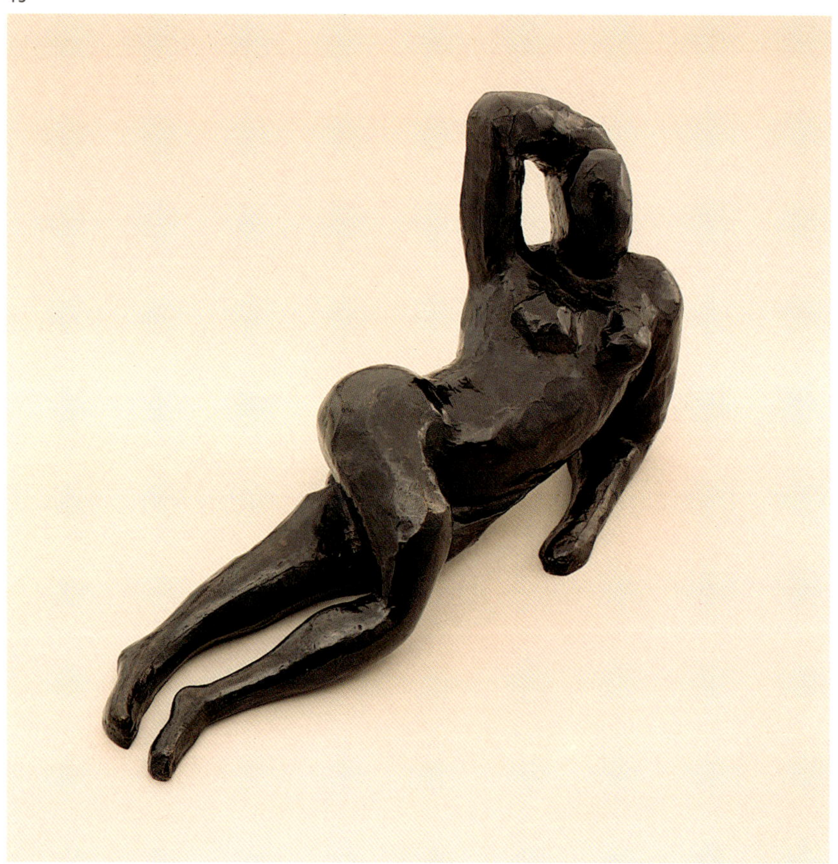

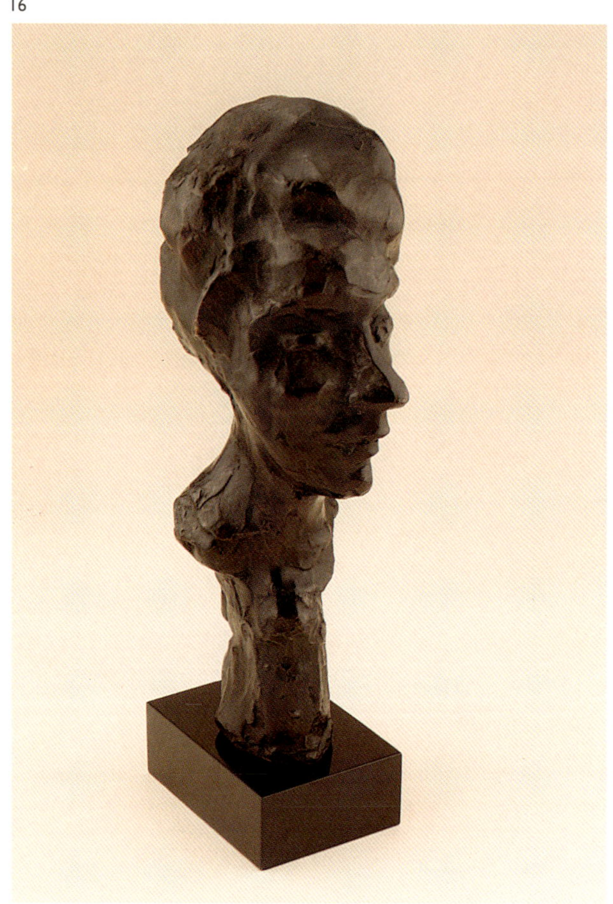

15 **Reclining Nude II**, 1927
Bronze

16 **Head of Marguerite**, 1915
Bronze

17 **White Plumes**, 1919
Oil on canvas

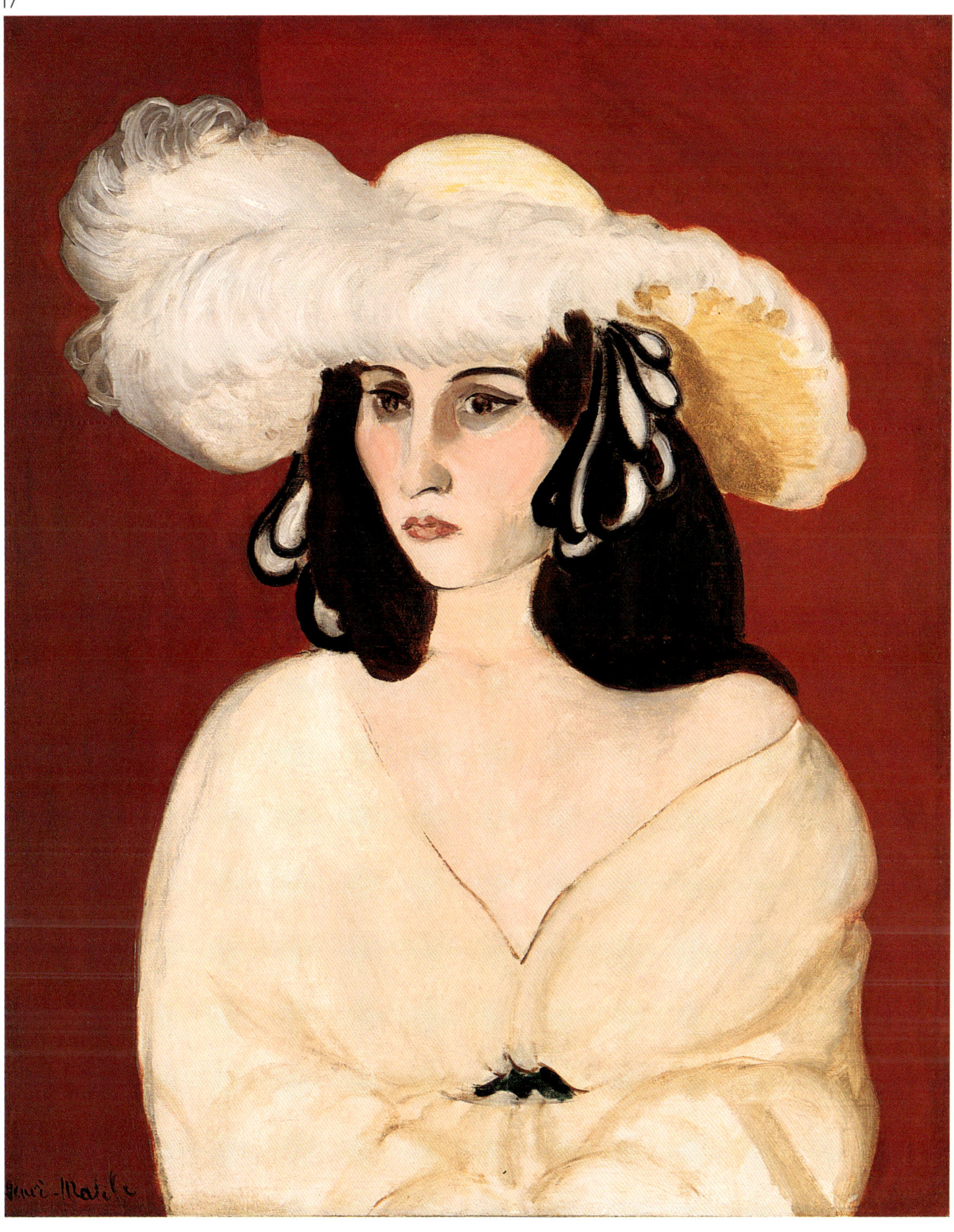

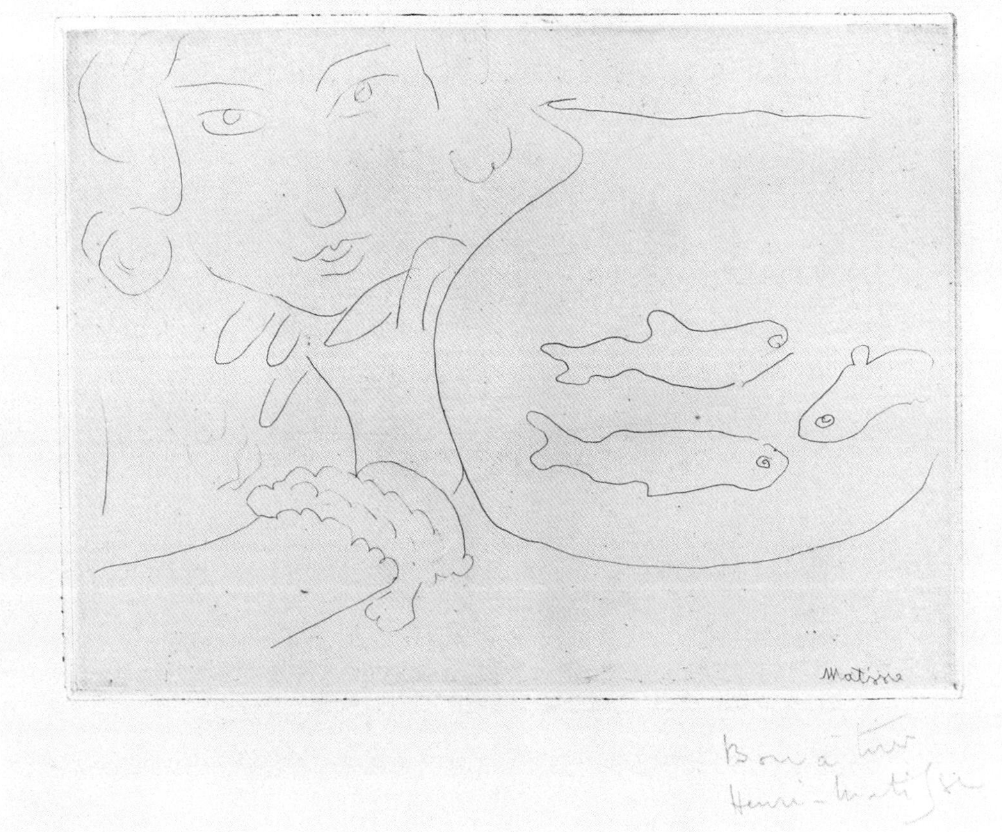

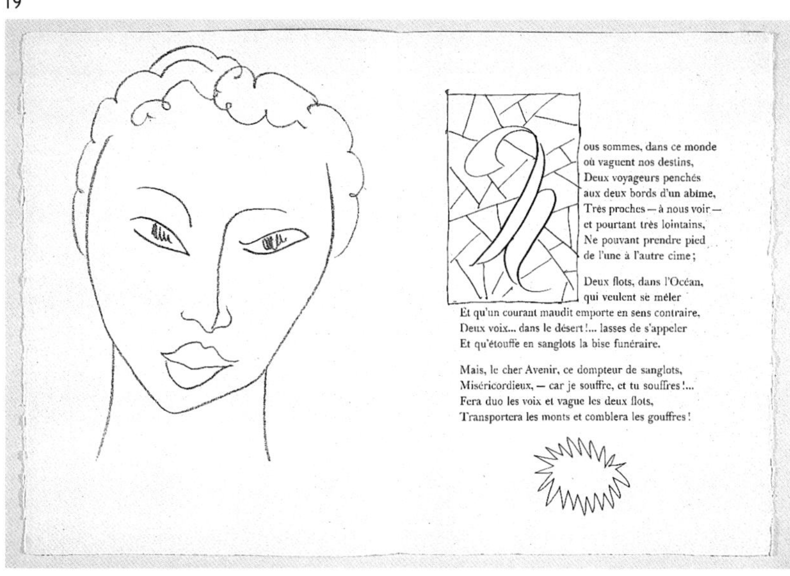

18 **Face of Young Woman and Bowl of Three Fish**, 1929
Etching

19 **Dedication**, from John-Antoine Nau's *Poésies antillaises*, 1972
Lithograph and reproductions of drawn ornaments

20 Frontispiece for **Pasiphaé, Chant de Minos**, 1943
Linoleum cut

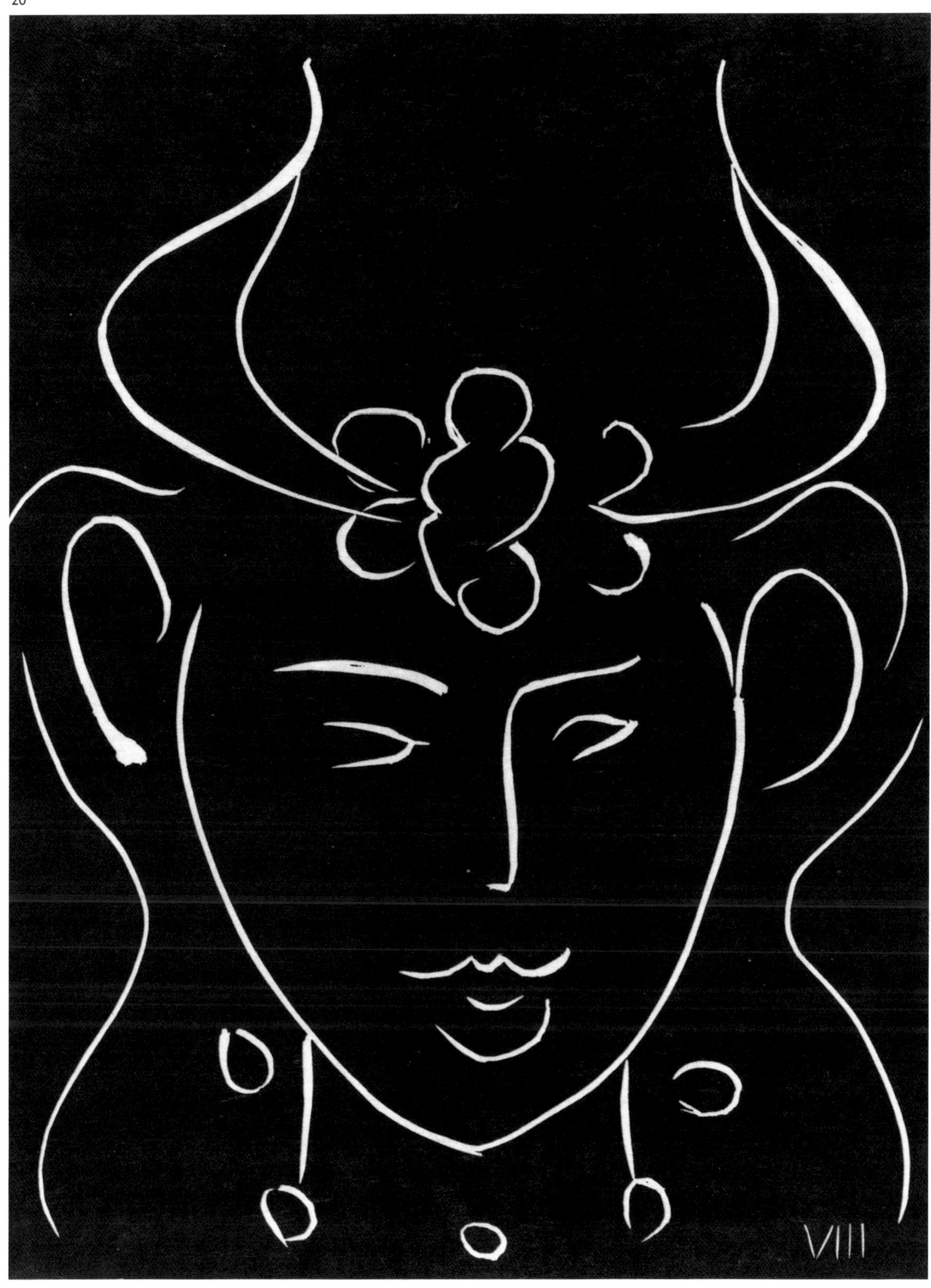
VIII

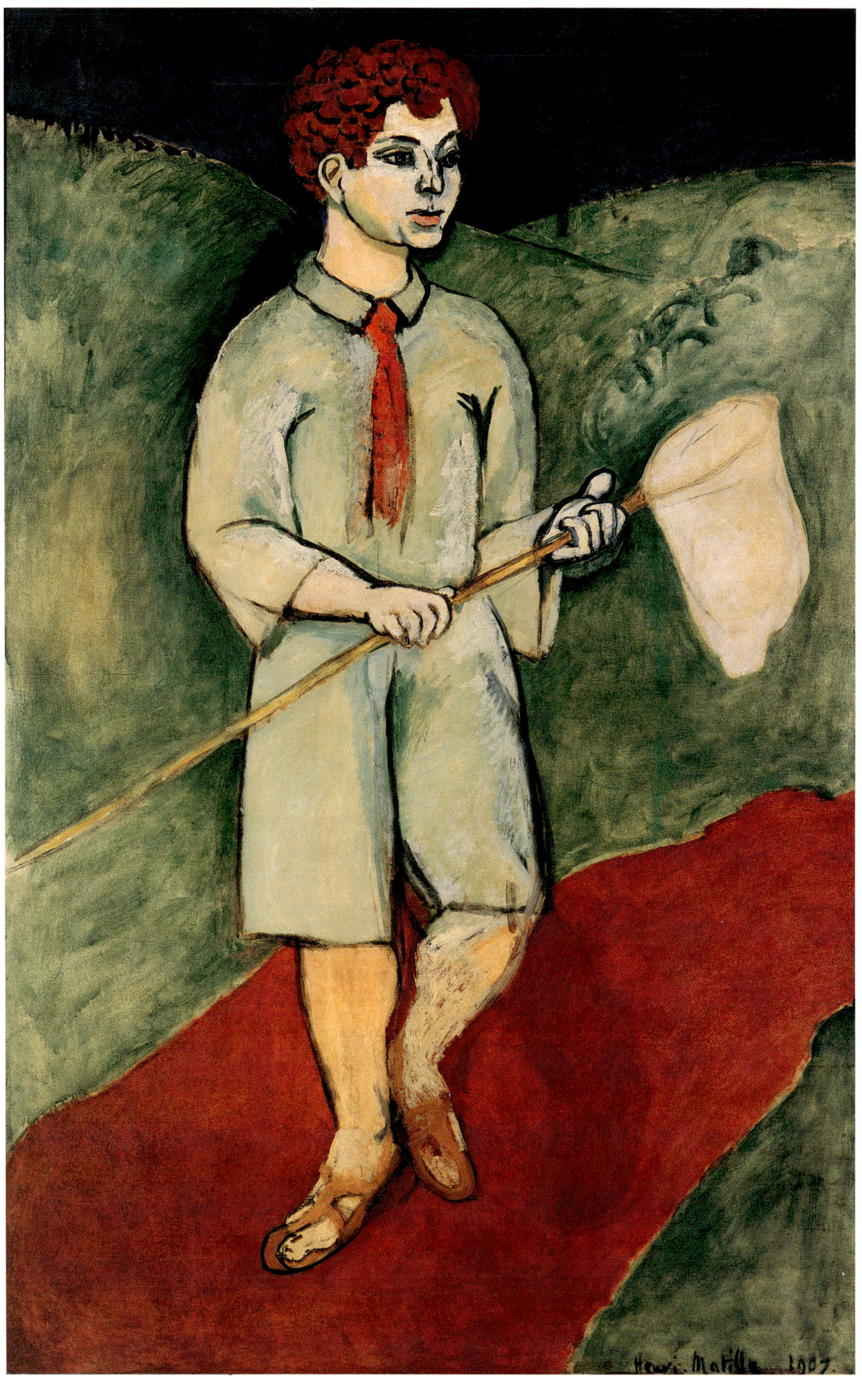

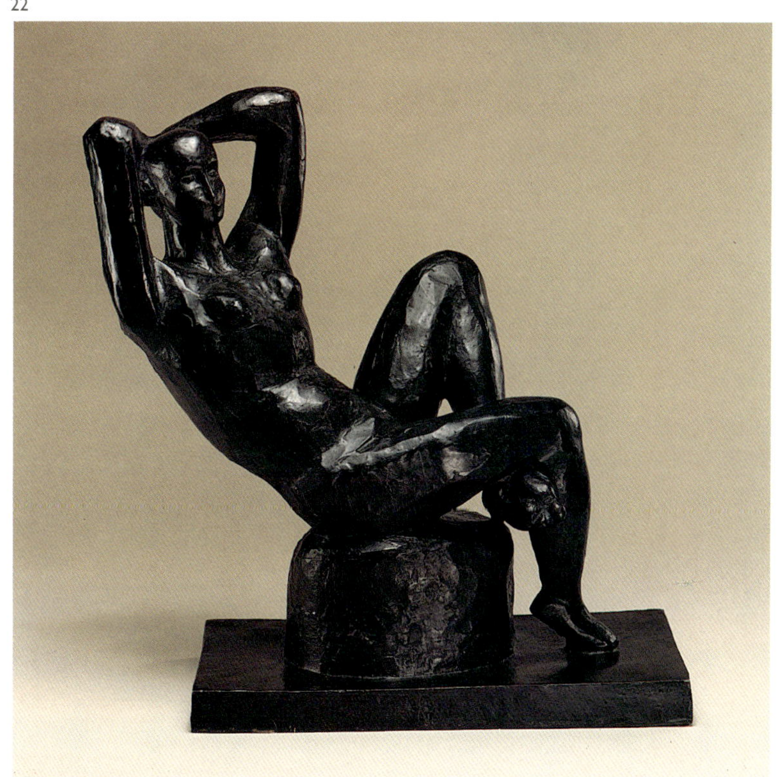

22

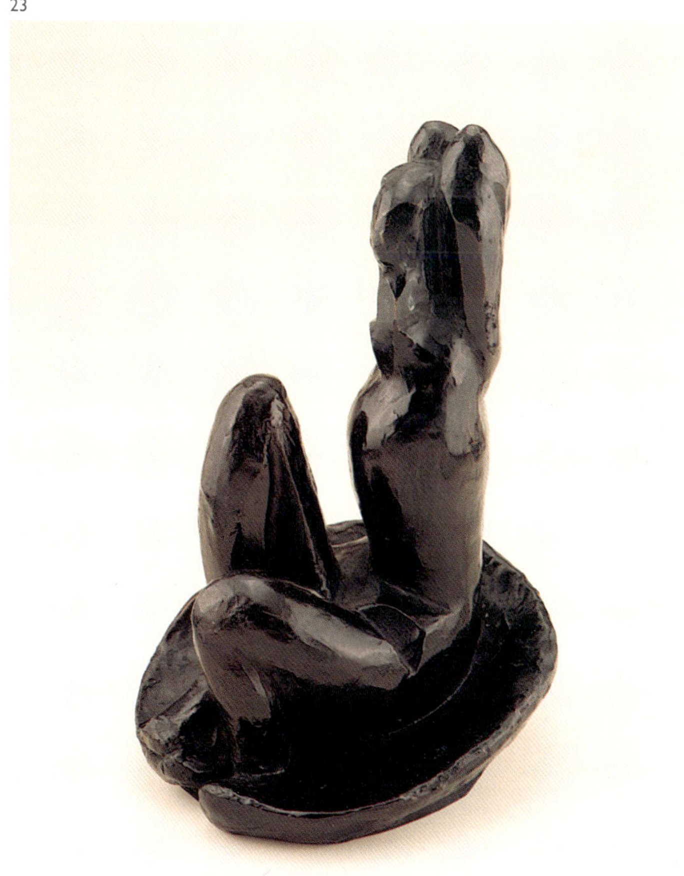

23

21 **Boy with a Butterfly Net**,
1907
Oil on canvas

22 **Large Seated Nude**, 1923–25
Bronze

23 **Venus in a Shell I**, 1930
Bronze

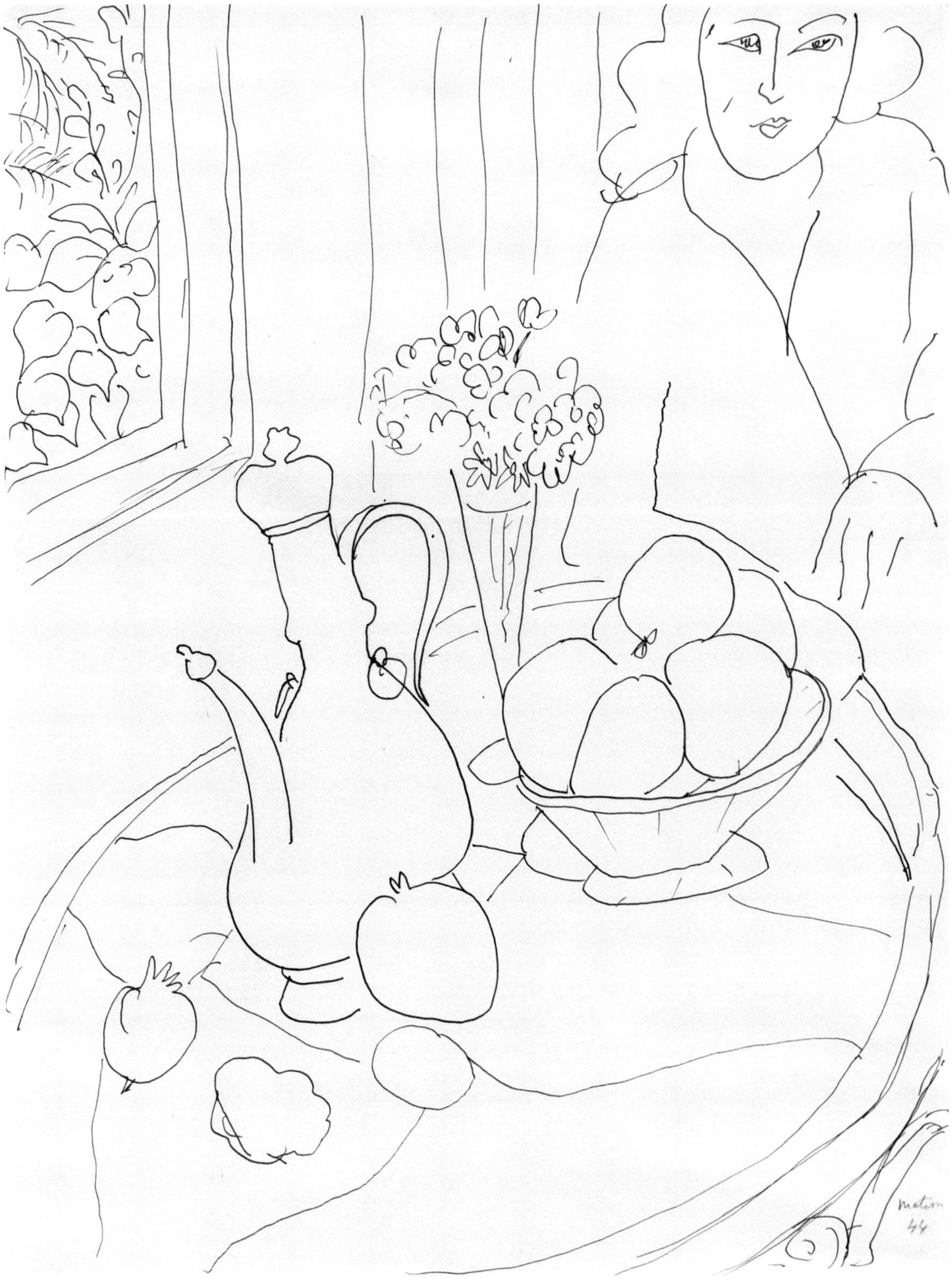

25

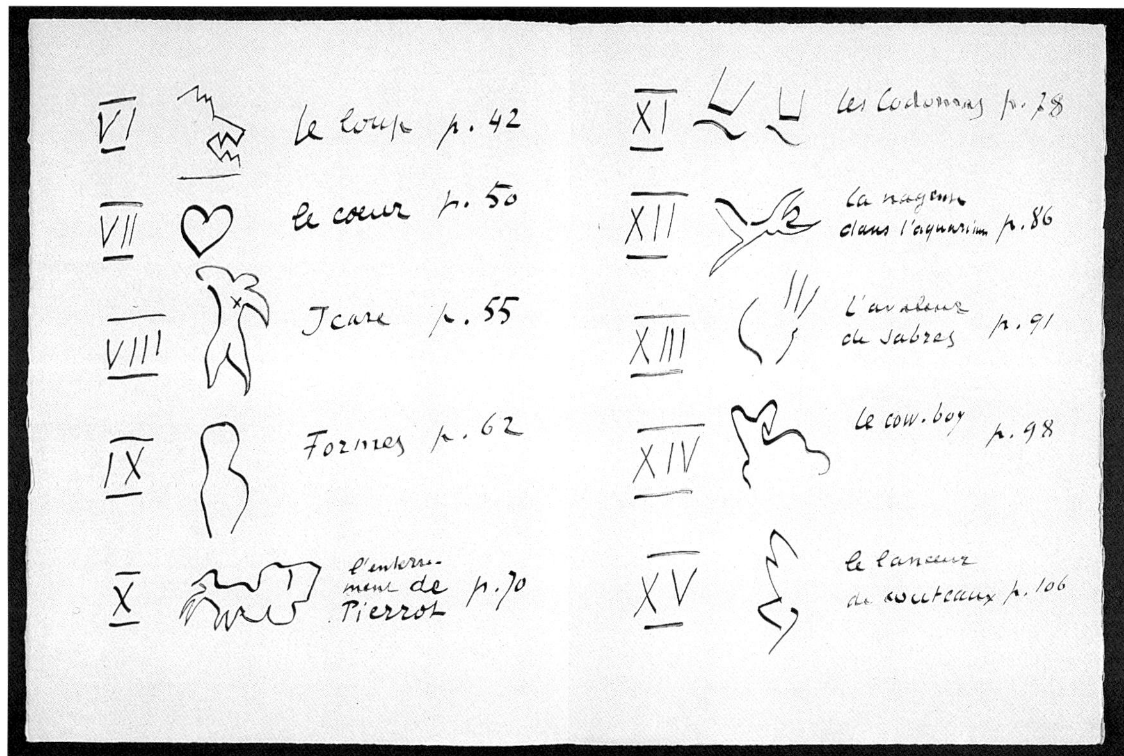

26

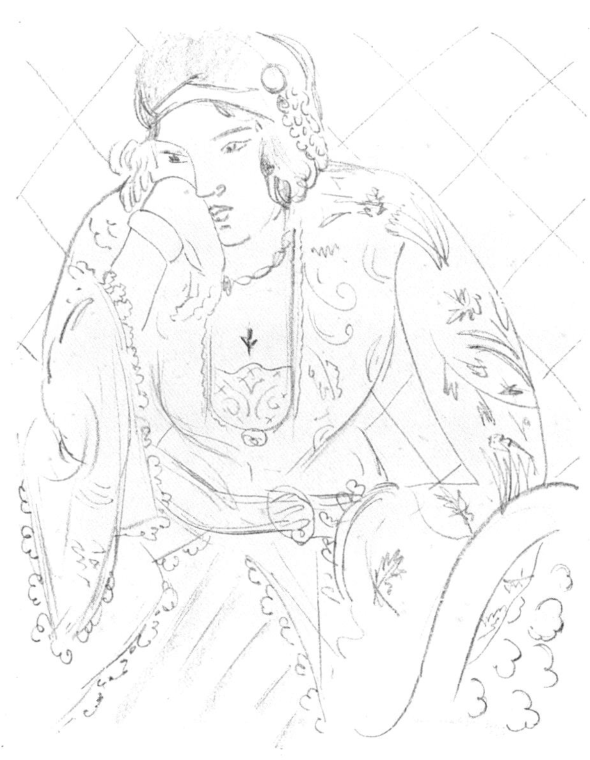

24 **Woman with Still Life**, 1944
    Pen and ink on paper

25 Pages from the **Table des
    Images**, from *Jazz*, 1947
    Reproductions of drawn script

26 **Woman with Trifoliate Cross**,
    1929
    Lithograph

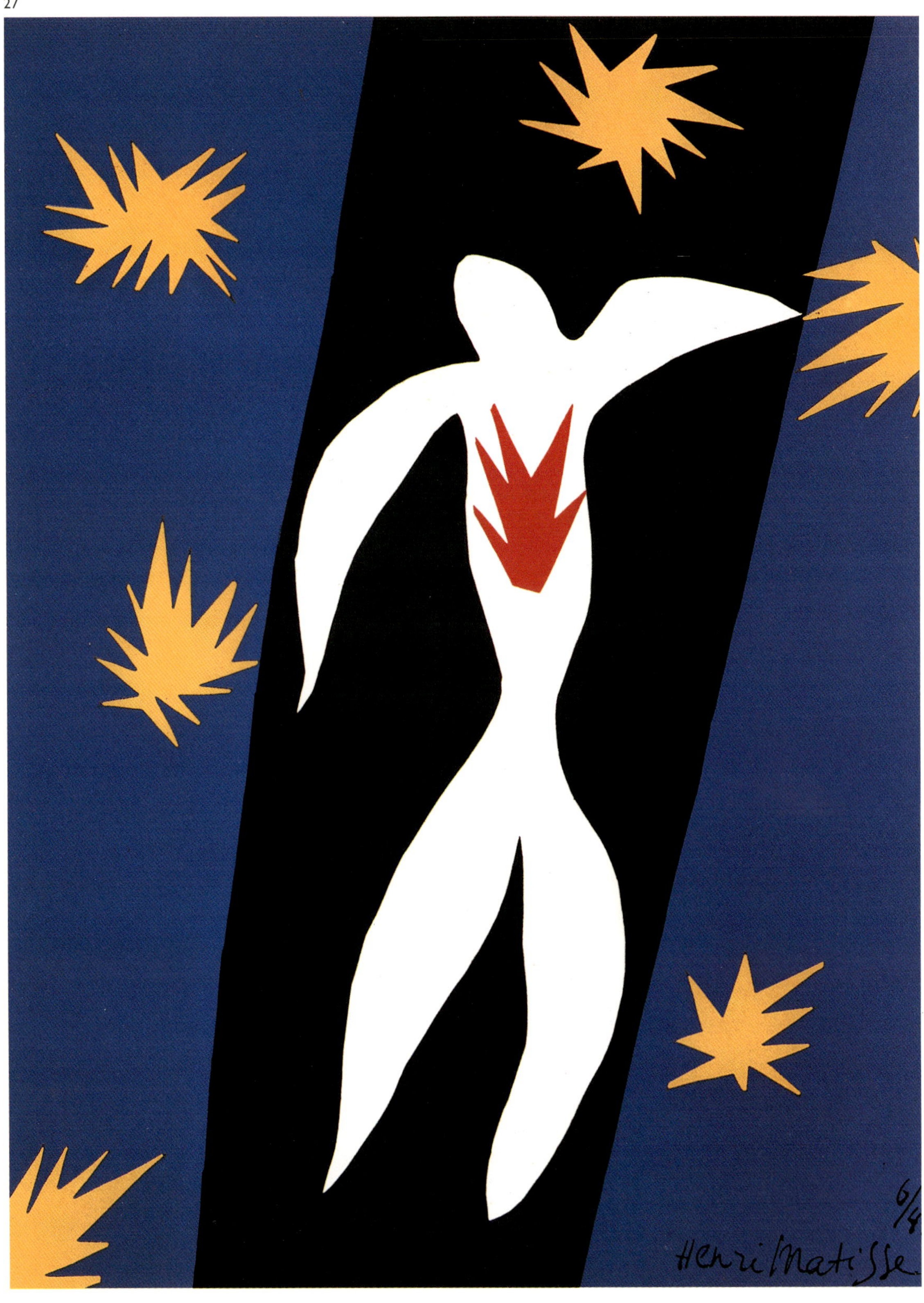

27 **Fall of Icarus**, frontispiece
from *Verve*, 1945
Lithographic reproduction of a
gouache cutout

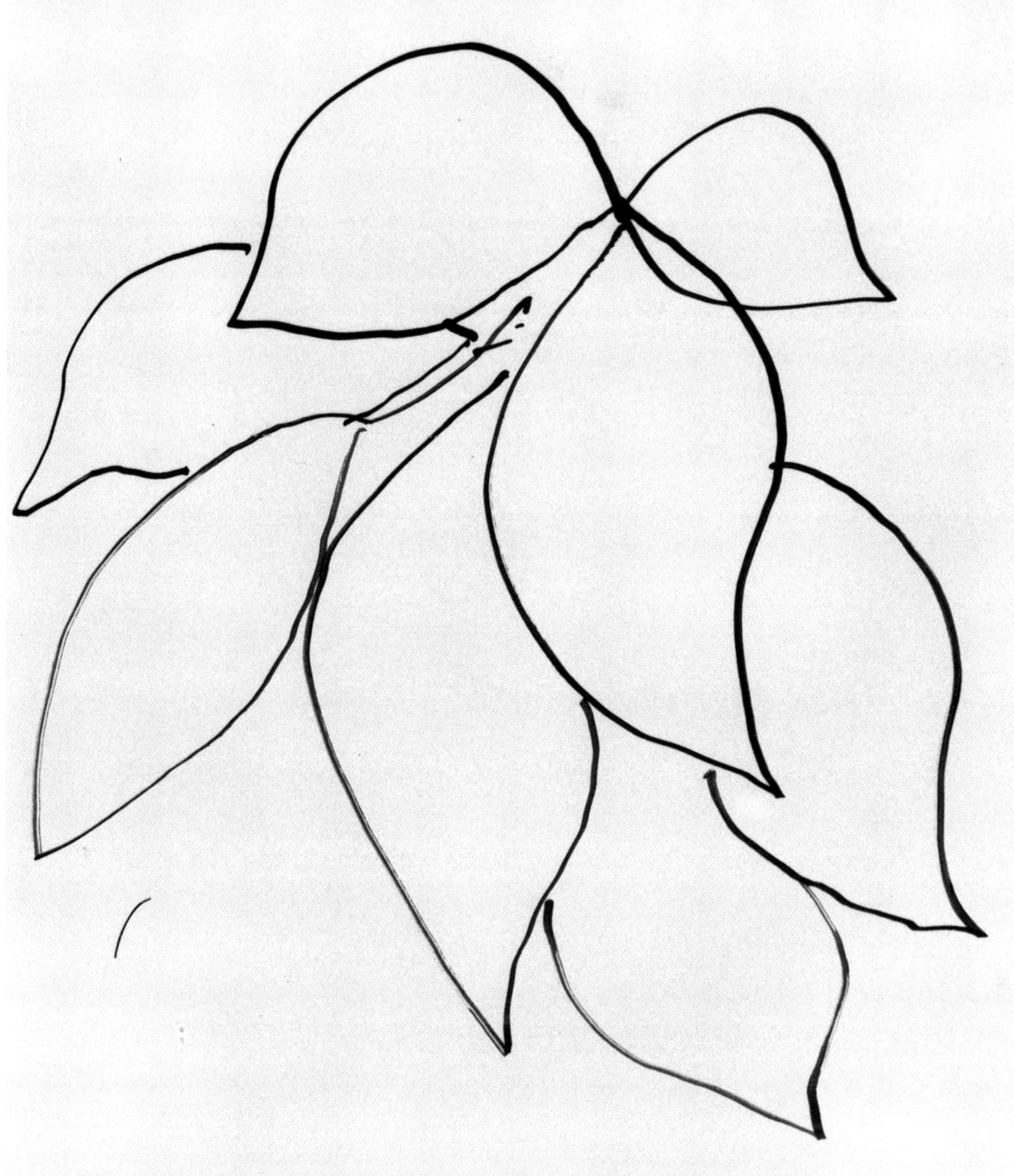

28 **Leaves**, 1948
Pen and ink on paper

Unless stated otherwise, objects are from the collection of The Minneapolis Institute of Arts. Each sculpture bears the foundry stamp: *CIRE /C. VALSUANI/ PERDUE*; all were given to the MIA by the Dayton Hudson Corporation in 1971. Unless otherwise indicated, the annotations on all works on paper are in graphite. Height precedes width and depth in the measurements provided for each object.

Catalog references: Duthuit-Matisse, Marguerite, and Claude Duthuit, *Henri Matisse: Catalogue raisonné de l'oeuvre gravé*, 2 vols. (Paris: [Claude Duthuit], 1983) and Duthuit, Claude, *Henri Matisse: Catalogue raisonné des ouvrages illustrés* (Paris: [Claude Duthuit], 1988).

Paintings

1   *Three Bathers*, 1907
      Oil on canvas, 24 x 29 in
      Signed at lower left: *Henri-Matisse*
      Bequest of Putnam Dana McMillan
2   *Music (Sketch)*, 1907
      Oil on canvas, 29 x 24 in
      Signed at lower left: *Henri Matisse*
      Museum of Modern Art, New York, gift of A. Conger Goodyear
        in honor of Alfred H. Barr, Jr.
3   *Boy with a Butterfly Net*, 1907
      Oil on canvas, 69¾ x 45⁵⁄₁₆ in
      Signed and dated at lower right: *Henri-Matisse 1907.*
      The Ethel Morrison Van Derlip Fund
4   *Interior with a Violin Case*, 1918–19
      Oil on canvas, 28¾ x 23½ in
      Signed at lower right: *Henri-Matisse*
      Museum of Modern Art, New York, Lillie P. Bliss Collection
5   *White Plumes*, 1919
      Oil on canvas, 28¾ x 23⅝ in
      Signed at lower left: *Henri-Matisse*
      The William Hood Dunwoody Fund
6   *Still Life with "Pensées" by Pascal*, 1924
      Oil on canvas, 19⅜ x 25½ in
      Signed at lower left: *Henri-Matisse*
      Collection of Ruth and Bruce Dayton

Sculpture

7   *Madeleine I*, 1901
      Bronze, 23½ x 9 x 7½ in
      Signed and numbered on base: *Henri-Matisse Nº 6*
8   *Head of Marguerite*, 1915
      Bronze, 12⅞ x 4¼ x 5½ in
      Initialed and numbered on lower back: *HM/7*
9   *Large Seated Nude*, 1923–25
      Bronze, 31 x 32 x 13¾ in
      Initialed and numbered on lower back: *HM/2*
10   *Reclining Nude II*, 1927
      Bronze, 11 x 19⅛ x 7½ in
      Numbered on lower back: *Nº 8*
11   *Venus in a Shell I*, 1930
      Bronze, 12½ x 8 x 7½ in
      Numbered on lower back: *N.6*

Drawings

12   *Woman with Folded Hands*, about 1919
      Pen and ink on wove paper, 10⅝ x 14⅜ in
      Signed at lower right: *Henri-Matisse*
      The John De Laittre Fund
13   *Reclining Nude*, about 1920
      Pencil on wove paper, 9¾ x 12¹¹⁄₁₆ in
      Signed at lower right: *Henri-Matisse*
      Private collection
14   *The Music Lesson*, about 1922
      Lithographic crayon on laid paper, 18⅜ x 24½ in
      Signed at lower right: *Henri-Matisse*
      Bequest of Putnam Dana McMillan
15   *Woman with Still Life*, 1944
      Pen and ink on wove paper, 20¾ x 15⅞ in
      Signed and dated at lower right: *Matisse/44*
      Gift of Ruth and Bruce Dayton
16   *Leaves*, 1948
      Pen and ink on coated wove paper, 13 x 9½ in
      Signed and dated at lower right, in ink: *H. Matisse 49*
      Gift of Ruth and Bruce Dayton

Prints

17   *Standing Nude Reader in Profile*, 1913
      Monogrammed lithograph on Japanese paper (Duthuit-Matisse 408)
      Image: 19⅝ x 10⁵⁄₁₆ in; sheet: 19¹³⁄₁₆ x 13 in
      Signed and numbered at lower right, in ink: *Henri-Matisse/19/50*
      Collection of Ruth and Bruce Dayton
18   *Seated Nude Seen from Back*, 1913
      Monogrammed lithograph on Japanese paper (Duthuit-Matisse 412)
      Image: 16⅝ x 10⅞ in; sheet: 19¹³⁄₁₆ x 13 in
      Numbered at lower right, in ink: *44/50*
      Private collection
19   *Three Apples and a Plate*, 1914/15
      Monotype on wove paper (Duthuit-Matisse 340)
      Plate mark: 3⅝ x 5⅝ in; sheet: 10⁵⁄₁₆ x 14⁵⁄₁₆ in
      The Putnam Dana McMillan Fund
20   *Standing Odalisque with a Plate of Fruit*, 1924
      Lithograph on Japanese paper (Duthuit-Matisse 444)
      Image: 14¾ x 10¹⁵⁄₁₆ in; sheet: 18¾ x 12⅞ in
      Numbered and signed at lower left and right: *3/10 Henri-*
        Matisse ep. d'artiste; Henri-Matisse
      Gift of Ruth and Bruce Dayton
21   *Seated Nude in a Floral-Decorated Armchair*, 1924
      Lithograph on Chinese paper (Duthuit-Matisse 445; Duthuit 44)
      Image: 18⅝ x 12½ in; sheet: 22¾ x 15¾ in
      Numbered and signed at lower left and right: *59/250;*
        Henri-Matisse
      The William Hood Dunwoody Fund, by exchange
22   *Large Odalisque in Bayadere Pantaloons*, 1925
      Lithograph on Chinese paper (Duthuit-Matisse 455)
      Image: 21⅛ x 17⅛ in; sheet: 29½ x 22⅛ in
      Signed and numbered at lower right: *Henri-Matisse 47/50*
      Private collection
23   *Seated Nude in a Tulle Shirt*, 1925
      Lithograph on Chinese paper (Duthuit-Matisse 465)
      Image: 14½ x 10¹⁵⁄₁₆ in; sheet: 21¹¹⁄₁₆ x 14¾ in
      Signed and numbered at lower right: *Henri-Matisse 6/50*
      Gift of Ruth and Bruce Dayton
24   *Odalisque with Dish of Fruit*, 1925
      Lithograph on Chinese paper (Duthuit-Matisse 466)
      Image: 13⁵⁄₁₆ x 10¼ in; sheet: 18¾ x 12⅞ in
      Signed and numbered at lower right: *Henri-Matisse 6/50*
      Gift of Ruth and Bruce Dayton
25   *Reclining Ballet Dancer* (from the album *Dix danseuses*,
        published in 1927), 1925/26
      Lithograph on Arches paper (Duthuit-Matisse 485)
      Image: 11 x 18⅜ in; sheet: 13 x 19⅝ in
      Numbered and signed at lower left: *111/130/Henri-Matisse*
      Walker Art Center, Minneapolis, gift of Judy and Kenneth
        Dayton
26   *Nude with Left Hand near Shoulder*, 1926
      Lithograph on Japanese paper (Duthuit-Matisse 474)
      Image: 17⅞ x 21¼ in; sheet: 18⅜ x 22⅞ in
      Numbered and signed at lower left and right: *8/50;*
        Henri-Matisse
      Walker Art Center, Minneapolis, Art Center Acquisition Fund
27   *Odalisque, Brazier, and Dish of Fruit*, 1929
      Lithograph on Arches paper (Duthuit-Matisse 504)
      Image: 10¹⁵⁄₁₆ x 14¹³⁄₁₆ in; sheet: 14¹⁵⁄₁₆ x 19¾ in
      Numbered and signed at lower right: *25/100/Henri-Matisse*
      Gift of Ruth and Bruce Dayton
28   *Seated Odalisque in a Moorish Chair*, 1929
      Lithograph on Arches paper (Duthuit-Matisse 508)
      Image: 11⅜ x 14⅛ in; sheet: 15½ x 19¹¹⁄₁₆ in
      Numbered and signed at lower right: *35/50/Henri-Matisse*
      The William Hood Dunwoody Fund, by exchange
29   *Figure before African Tapa Cloth*, 1929
      Lithograph on Japanese paper (Duthuit-Matisse 515)
      Image: 21 x 17 in; sheet: 25½ x 19¾ in
      Signed and numbered at lower right: *Henri-Matisse/28/50*
      Walker Art Center, Minneapolis, Art Center Acquisition Fund
30   *Woman with Trifoliate Cross*, 1929
      Lithograph on Arches paper (Duthuit-Matisse 516)
      Image: 21⅜ x 17⅛ in; sheet: 26⅛ x 19⅜ in
      Signed and numbered at lower right: *Henri-Matisse 32/50*
      Gift of Richard L. Hillstrom in memory of his parents, Martin
        and Alma Hillstrom
31   *Face with Pearl Necklace*, 1929
      Etching with surface tone on *chine-collé* on Arches paper
        (Duthuit-Matisse 136)
      Plate mark: 6⅜ x 4¹¹⁄₁₆ in; support: 15⁵⁄₁₆ x 11⅝ in
      Numbered and signed at lower right: *8/15/Henri-Matisse*
      Bequest of Kenneth R. Smith
32   *Face of Young Woman and Bowl of Three Fish*, 1929
      Etching with surface tone on *chine-collé* on Arches paper; one
        of two trial proofs (Duthuit-Matisse 169)
      Plate mark: 3⅜ x 4¹¹⁄₁₆ in; support: 11 x 14⁵⁄₁₆ in
      Inscribed at lower right: *Matisse*; signed at lower right: *Bon à*
        tirer/Henri-Matisse
      The Margaret McMillan Webber Estate, by exchange
33–38   Six illustrations for an edition of James Joyce's *Ulysses*
        published in New York in 1935 by the Limited Editions
        Club, 1934
      (33) *The Calypso Episode*
      (34) *Aeolus, Cave of the Winds*
      (35) *The Cyclops*
      (36) *The Episode of Nausicaä*

(37) *The Circe Episode*
(38) *Symbolic Landscape: Ithaca*
Soft-ground etchings on wove paper (Duthuit 6; Duthuit-
    Matisse 235–40)
Plate mark: about 11½ x 9 in; sheet: about 16½ x 12½ in
Each numbered and signed at lower left and right: *102/150;
    Henri-Matisse*
Frederick R. Weisman Art Museum, University of Minnesota,
    Minneapolis

39 *Bowl of Begonias I*, 1938
Linoleum cut on G. Maillol paper (Duthuit-Matisse 718)
Plate mark: 7⅞ x 9¹⁄₁₆ in; sheet: 15¹¹⁄₁₆ x 17⅝ in
Numbered and signed at lower right: *24/25/Henri Matisse*
Miscellaneous purchase funds, by exchange

40 *Nude with Bracelet*, 1940
Linoleum cut on Arches paper (Duthuit-Matisse 725)
Plate mark: 9⁹⁄₁₆ x 7 in; sheet: 17⅛ x 12⁹⁄₁₆ in
Signed and numbered at lower right: *H. Matisse/10/10*
Collection of Ruth and Bruce Dayton

41 Rejected frontispiece for *Pasiphaé, Chant de Minos*, 1943
Linoleum cut on Chinese paper (Duthuit 10)
Plate mark: 10⁷⁄₁₆ x 7¹⁵⁄₁₆ in; sheet: 13 x 9⅝ in
Inscribed at lower right: *VIII*
The Margaret McMillan Webber Estate, by exchange

42–43 Two female portraits for *Poésies antillaises*, 1945–46
Lithographs on Japanese and Arches paper (Duthuit 37)
Sheet: about 15 x 11½ in
Collection of Ruth and Bruce Dayton

44 *Catherinette*, 1946
Lithograph on *chine-collé* on Arches paper (Duthuit-
    Matisse 620)
Image: 10½ x 8⁹⁄₁₆ in; support: 19⅝ x 15⁵⁄₁₆ in
Signed and numbered at lower left: *H Matisse/3/100*
Bequest of Mrs. Charles S. Pillsbury

45 *Madonna and Child*, 1949
Lithographic reproduction of an ink drawing relating to
    Matisse's ceramic mural, *Madonna and Child*, at the Chapel
    at Vence
Sheet: 9¼ x 15⅝ in
Signed at lower right, in ink: *H. Matisse*
Collection of Ruth and Bruce Dayton

46 *Marie-José in a Yellow Dress*, 1950
Colored aquatint on Arches paper (Duthuit-Matisse 817)
Plate mark: 22⅞ x 16⅜ in; sheet: 30 x 22⁷⁄₁₆ in
Signed and numbered at lower right: *H. Matisse/25/100*
Private collection (formerly collection of Donald Winston)

Illustrated Books

47 Stéphane Mallarmé. *Poésies*. Lausanne: Albert Skira, 1932
Etchings: executed 1931–32
Format 13³⁄₁₆ x 9⅞ in, unbound (Duthuit 5)
Copy 42, signed: *Henri-Matisse*
Gift of Bruce B. Dayton

48 *Paris 1937: Textes et gravures.* Texts by Paul Valéry,
    et al. Paris: Daragnès, 1937
Etching, *La Cité—Notre-Dame*: executed 1936–37
Format 13¾ x 10⅝ in, unbound (Duthuit 7; Duthuit-
    Matisse 248)
Etching inscribed at lower right, in reverse: *Matisse*
Gift of Ruth and Bruce Dayton

49 Henry de Montherlant. *Pasiphaé, Chant de Minos*. Paris:
    Martin Fabiani, [1944]
Linoleum cuts: executed 1942–43
Format 13³⁄₁₆ x 10⅛ in, unbound (Duthuit 10)
Copy xx, signed in ink: *Henri Matisse*
Gift of Bruce B. Dayton

50 *Verve. Henri Matisse: De la couleur*, vol. IV, no. 13. Paris, 1945
Cover, title page, and frontispiece based on artist's original
    gouache cutouts: executed 1943
Format 14 x 10⁷⁄₁₆ in, bound (Duthuit 74 and 104)
Gift of Ruth and Bruce Dayton

51 Henri Matisse. *Visages*. [Paris]: Éditions du Chêne, [1946]
Lithographs, linoleum cuts, and initials: executed 1944–45
Format 13⅜ x 10⁵⁄₁₆ in, unbound (Duthuit 11)
Copy 155, signed: *Henri Matisse*
Gift of Bruce B. Dayton

52 Marianna Alcaforado. *Lettres [portugaises]*. Paris: Tériade,
    [1946]
Lithographs: executed 1945
Format 10¹³⁄₁₆ x 8¼ in, unbound (Duthuit 15)
Copy 61, signed in ink: *H. Matisse*
Gift of Bruce B. Dayton

53 *Pierre à feu. Les miroirs profonds*, no. 2. Comp. Jacques
    Kober. Paris: Maeght, 1947
Linoleum cut; cover, based on artist's original gouache cutout,
    and lithograph: executed 1941 and 1947
Format 9⅝ x 8¼ in, bound (Duthuit 17)
Copy 719
Gift of Ruth and Bruce Dayton

54 Charles Baudelaire. *Les fleurs du mal*. [Paris]: Bibliothèque
    Française, [1947]
Photolithographs; etching and ornaments: executed 1944 and
    1946
Format 11¼ x 9⁵⁄₁₆ in, bound (Duthuit 19)
Copy 286, signed: *H. Matisse*
Gift of Ruth and Bruce Dayton

55 André Rouveyre. *Repli*. [Paris]: Bélier, [1947]
Cover based on artist's original gouache cutout, lithographs,
    and linoleum cuts: executed 1946–47
Format 10⅛ x 6⅝ in, unbound (Duthuit 20)
Copy 72, signed: *H Matisse*
Gift of Ruth and Bruce Dayton

56 Henri Matisse. *Jazz*. [Paris]: Tériade, [1947]
Colored plates from artist's original gouache cutouts; original
    text and ornaments based on those drawn by the artist:
    executed 1943–44 and 1946
Format 16¾ x 12¹³⁄₁₆ in, unbound (Duthuit 22)
Copy 83, signed: *H Matisse*
Gift of Bruce B. Dayton

57a & 57b Pierre de Ronsard. *Florilège des Amours*. Paris: Albert Skira,
    [1948]
Lithographs: executed 1941–48
Format 15¼ x 11⅜ in, unbound (Duthuit 25)
Copies 256 and 195, each signed in ink: *H. Matisse*
Copy number 256: Gift of Bruce B. Dayton
Copy number 195: Collection of Ruth and Bruce Dayton

58 *Verve. Vence 1944–48*, vol. VI, nos. 21 and 22. Paris, 1948
Cover and frontispiece based on artist's original gouache
    cutouts: executed 1948
Format 14 x 10⁷⁄₁₆ in, bound (Duthuit 84 and 108)
Gift of Ruth and Bruce Dayton

59a & 59b Charles d'Orléans. *Poèmes*. [Paris]: Tériade, [1950]
Lithographic reproductions of colored-crayon drawings and
    text drawn by the artist: executed 1942–49
Format 16¼ x 10⅜ in, unbound (Duthuit 28)
Copies 674 and 831, each signed: *H. Matisse*
Copy number 674: Gift of Bruce B. Dayton
Copy number 831: Frederick R. Weisman Art Museum,
    University of Minnesota, Minneapolis

60 André Rouveyre. *Apollinaire*. Paris: Raisons d'Être, [1952]
Lithographs; cover and jacket based on artist's original
    gouache cutouts, aquatint, and linoleum cuts: executed
    1944 and 1950–52
Format 12⅜ x 10³⁄₁₆ in , unbound (Duthuit 31)
Copy 226
Gift of Ruth and Bruce Dayton

61 Henri Matisse. *Portraits*. Monte-Carlo: André Sauret–Éditions
    du Livre, 1954
Lithograph; cover based on artist's original gouache cutout:
    executed 1951 and 1953
Format 12⁷⁄₁₆ x 9⅜ in, bound (Duthuit 33)
Copy 1291
Gift of Ruth and Bruce Dayton

62 *Verve. Dernières oeuvres de Matisse 1950–1954*, vol. IX,
    nos. 35 and 36. Paris, 1958
Cover based on artist's original gouache cutout: executed
    1954
Format 14 x 10⁷⁄₁₆ in, bound (Duthuit 139)
Gift of Ruth and Bruce Dayton

63 Georges Duthuit. *Une fête en Cimmérie*. Paris: Tériade, 1963
Lithographs: executed 1948–50
Format 10 x 7⅞ in, unbound (Duthuit 35)
Copy 43
Gift of Ruth and Bruce Dayton

64 John-Antoine Nau. *Poésies antillaises*. [Paris]: Fernand
    Mourlot, 1972
Lithographs and ornaments: executed 1945–53
Format 15⁵⁄₁₆ x 11½ in, unbound (Duthuit 37)
Copy 207
Gift of Bruce B. Dayton

65 Henri Matisse. *Gravures originales sur les thèmes de "Chant
    de Minos" et "Pasiphaé."* 2 vols. Paris: [artist's heirs], 1981
Rejected linoleum cuts for Henry de Montherlant's 1944
    Pasiphaé (see cat. no. 49): executed 1943
Format 13³⁄₁₆ x 10³⁄₁₆ in, unbound (Duthuit 38 and 38 bis)
Copy 95
Gift of Bruce B. Dayton

This book was produced in conjunction with the
exhibition "Minnesota Celebrates Matisse," held at
The Minneapolis Institute of Arts, October 10, 1993,
to January 9, 1994.

Designed by Jill MacTaggart Blumer
Edited by Susan C. Jones
Photographs by Gary Mortensen and Robert Fogt
Typeset by Lynne Cason

Library of Congress Catalog Card Number 93-86271
International Standard Book Number 0-912964-52-9

"Minnesota Celebrates Matisse" is made possible
through the support of Robins, Kaplan, Miller &
Ciresi and The Donald Winston Exhibition Fund.
Promotional support is being provided by Target
Stores.

Cover illustrations:
Destiny and **Wolf**, from *Jazz*, 1947
Stencil reproductions of gouache cutouts